Hands on History

Rebecca Carnihan

Acknowledgements

The author and publisher would like to thank Headteacher Mrs C Eubank, Deputy Headteacher Miss C Keen, all staff and especially the children of Grinling Gibbons Primary School in Deptford, London for their hard work, enthusiasm and pride in the production of work for this book.

We would also like to thank Art Teacher Rachel Bull and the children at St Stephen's C of E Primary School, in New Cross, London for their fantastic contribution to the book.

A very special thank you is given to Hilary Carnihan, who is ever-supportive, always encouraging and through her commitment was an outstanding help during the project. Thank you.

Roman People (page 30)

Belair Publications, Waterslade House, Thame Road, Haddenham, Buckinghamshire, HP17 NT.

Email: belair@belair-publications.co.uk

Commissioning Editor: Zoë Parish   Editor: Janice Baiton

Page Layout: Barbara Linton   Photography: Steve Forest   Cover Design: Steve West

First published in 2008 by Belair Publications.

British Library Cataloguing in Publication Data. A catalogue record for this publication is available from the British Library.

ISBN 978-1-84191-467-1

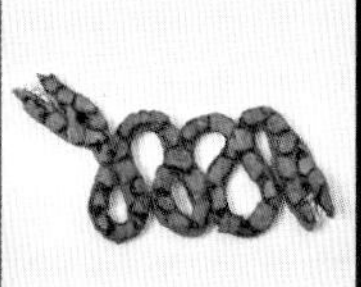

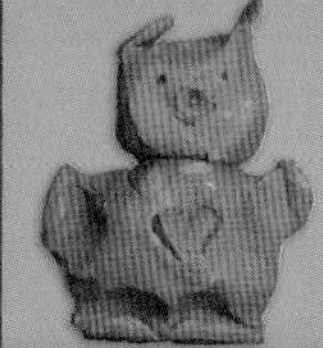

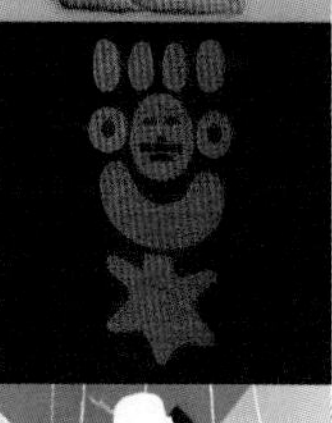

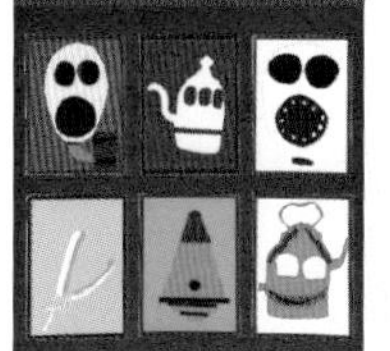

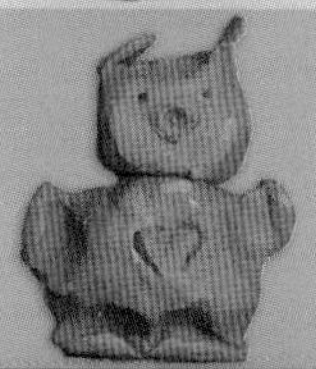
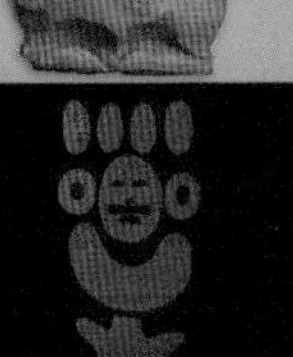
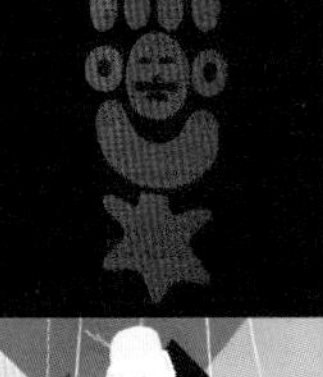

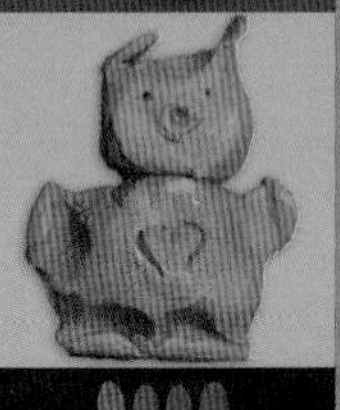

Contents

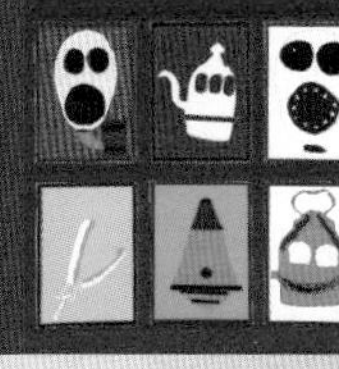

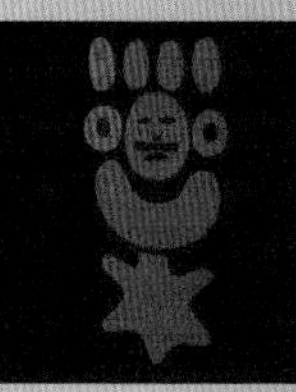

Introduction

In my experience as a primary art specialist I have found that history lends itself particularly well to visual art projects. This book contains a wide range of art activities and displays based upon popular primary history themes.

I have organised the contents of the bookapproximately in age order, starting with the projects for the youngest children, though there are many over lapping themes that can be adapted for different age groups. Themes can be 'dipped into' providing a new angle on the past.

History-based art activities help to deepen understanding of the subject and allow children to place themselves in a given context. They enable children to envisage life in another era and to understand the process by which artefacts were made.

The aim of each activity is for children to gain knowledge and understanding of themselves and the world around them, a sense of time and place, and an awareness of the ideas and ways of living of those in the past.

Where possible, encourage the children to contribute to the interpretation of a project and give them room to innovate. Thematic displays are great for the children to be proud of their work.

The majority of the activities are three-dimensional and staple artwork resources are used. Such resources are easily accessible and often free when recycled. One tip is to find out if there is a children's scrap project in your local area – they are usually charitable organisations that gather clean waste materials from light industries specifically for this use. Or contact your local council for a similar scheme.

I hope these activities prove useful and bring out the best in your children. They are there to provide a range of stimulating and creative opportunities that create a framework for success and enjoyment.

Rebecca Carnihan

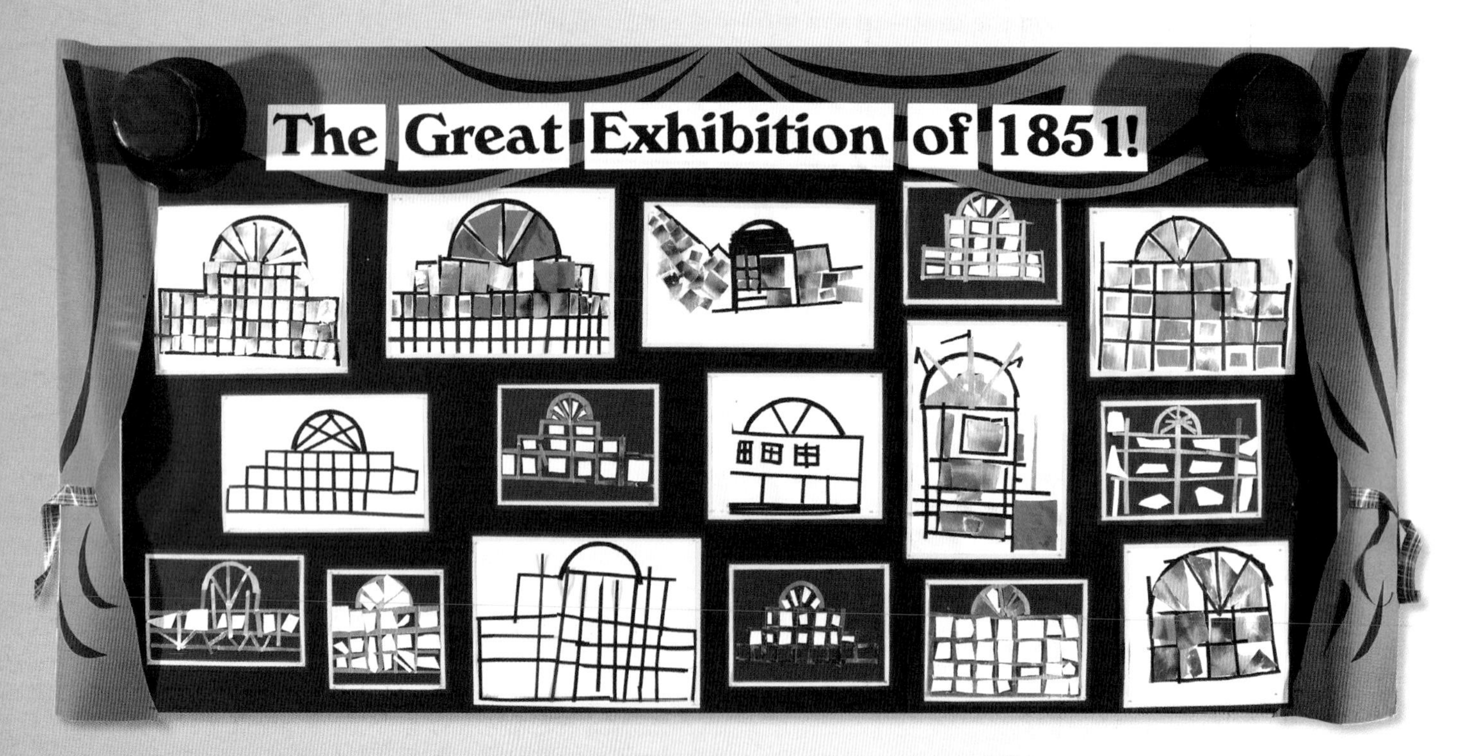

Crystal Palace and The Great Exhibition (page 38)

Terraced Houses

This project will take several sessions to complete. It combines many aspects of art, interior design and architecture and is good for helping young children to create their own world. The terraced house is both a Victorian and a contemporary project as it is a model many of us continue to inhabit. Begin by providing images of a terraced house and discuss the materials used (brick, metal railings, glass) and design features (pointed roof, chimney, lighting).

Approach

The exterior

1. Cut away two a-joining sides of the cardboard box to give four sides to form the front, ground floor and two sides of the house.
2. To create the front of the house, first draw windows and a door on the card.
3. Put the paint in a container wide enough to accommodate the squares being used for printing the bricks.
4. For the brick façade, dip the squares in paint and print from left to right to build up a brick texture on the front of the house. Allow to dry then stick the card onto the exterior of the box.
5. Draw on the windows, and cut out the frames with the cutting knife (adult only). On the reverse side, place the transparent plastic over the frame and stick in place using sellotape. Glue on the lolly sticks to form a doorframe.
6. To make the roof, score down the centre of the card and bend it in half (adult only). Bend to a point and attach to the top of the house using the glue gun or strong tape.
7. Cut out rectangular shapes and stick onto the card roof to look like tiles. Alternatively, use the printing method used for the brick façade but with larger rectangles and darker colours.

Resources

- Cardboard box

Brick façade

- Thin card A4 × 1
- Pencils
- Poster paint – red, orange, yellow
- Small squares/rectangles (e.g. balsa wood)
- Lolly sticks
- Cutting knife (adult use only)
- Coloured plastic (acetate, gel or sweet wrappers)

Roof

- Stiff card
- Glue stick
- Glue gun/or strong tape
- Coloured paper – brown, black, dark red

Interior

- Variety of small containers, packaging, balsa wood etc.
- White paper A4
- Poster paint

The interior

1. Make wallpaper by creating patterns with paint, for example, dots using fingers. Stick to the interior walls when dry.
2. Use the small containers and pieces of clean packaging to make furniture. Stick using PVA glue (a little masking tape may be needed to temporarily secure them in place).
3. Optional: include a photo of the child inside their built home – sleeping, washing up etc.

The Three Little Pigs

The story of the *Three Little Pigs* lends itself well to an exploration into the use of materials for building a home. It is also an opportunity for children to add a narrative to the work. The project is best completed over a few sessions to allow drying time for the different materials. It combines hay, wood and brick into one 'home'. Read a version of the story before starting the project and discuss the materials used in the three pigs' homes.

Resources

- Shoebox
- Hay or straw
- Lolly sticks or twigs
- Paper for bricks – brown, ochre, red, orange etc.
- Cotton wool or white tissue paper
- Coloured tissue paper
- Plasticine or painted clay
- Clay modelling tools
- PVA glue and spreaders
- Cardboard tube or paper

Approach

1. Cover the top and bottom of the shoebox with hay, applying plenty of PVA glue to the surface. It is an awkward task, so try to keep fingers as free of glue as possible and patiently press the hay to adhere.
2. Once the glue is dry, cover the right side, left side and back of the box with the lolly sticks or twigs (lolly sticks are easier to handle as they lie flat on the surface) to represent wood.
3. For the bricks, cut several rectangle shapes in 'brick' colours and stick them on the inside of the box.
4. For the chimney, cut a cardboard tube or make a tube shape from paper and stick this to the roof of the house. Add smoke using cotton wool or white tissue paper.
5. Make a small fire in the house using twigs and coloured tissue paper, and position directly under the chimney. A small cooking pot could be made of clay or plasticine to go onto the fire.
6. Using plasticine or clay, create the characters of the story. The three little pigs should sit inside the house, and the wolf should look as though he is about to climb down the chimney.

Finger Puppets

This project makes a good link with literacy. The main characters in any children's story can be brought to life using this simple device. This example uses *Little Red Riding Hood*. Although the puppets can be used in displays, they are at their best when used as toys in role-play activities.

Resources

- Coloured paper
- Paper
- Sellotape
- Scissors
- Wool
- Felt
- Card
- PVA glue

Approach

1. The basis for each puppet is a paper tube wrapped around the finger to fit and secured with sellotape.
2. For Red Riding Hood use red paper to create the tube, then cut two trapezium shapes for the hood and the skirt.
3. Draw Red Riding Hood's face on a circular piece of paper, cut out and stick to the top of the tube. Use pieces of wool for the hair and felt for the arms and legs. For the basket, cut out a small 'u' shape and glue or tape on a string handle.
4. For the wolf use a dark coloured card and dark wool for the body (as opposite), and dark felt for his legs. Use small pointed pieces of card for the teeth ears and claws.

Marionettes

This is good exercise in anatomy as well as for children crafting their own toy. Begin with a discussion about types of puppet (it is a good follow-on from making finger puppets). Show the children some examples of puppets including string puppets. Discuss how they work. Ask the children what they know about Pinocchio and read them the story. Talk about how Pinocchio was able to move in the story. Making a large diagram of the body is a good tool to explain the similarities between a marionette and the human body.

Resources

- Large sheet of paper or wallpaper strip
- Marker pen
- Thin card 40 × 20cm
- Hole punch
- Butterfly clips × 16 per puppet
- Lolly sticks
- Coloured pencils
- Coloured paper/collage materials
- String

Approach

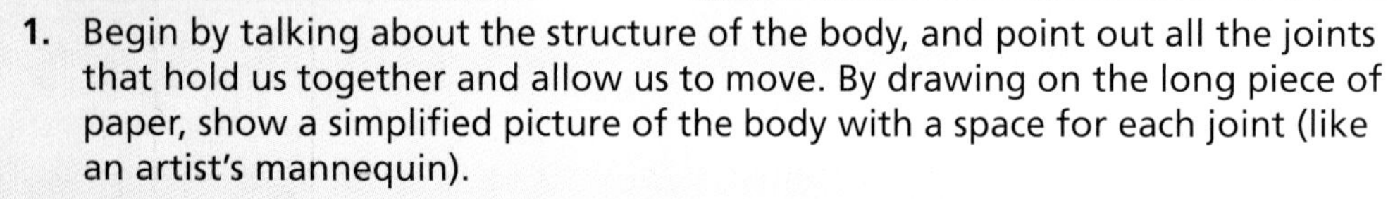

1. Begin by talking about the structure of the body, and point out all the joints that hold us together and allow us to move. By drawing on the long piece of paper, show a simplified picture of the body with a space for each joint (like an artist's mannequin).

2. Label each section: head, upper arm, lower arm etc.

3. Ask each child to draw a copy of the diagram on the card, taking care to keep the proportions and size as large as possible.
4. Cut out each piece and arrange on a table. Using the hole punch (best done by an adult), make holes where the joints will be. Put butterfly clips through the joints to assemble the body.
5. Glue two lolly sticks together in a crossed position. Tie one end of the string to the centre of the cross and the other to the puppet's head. Continue to attach the remaining strings to knees and hands.
6. Use coloured pencils and coloured paper/collage materials to decorate the puppet.

Teddy Bears

This classic and enduring toy that children continue to enjoy can be made in a 2-D form that explores texture and pattern. In this project, teddy is made up of separate pieces to allow movement and to help young children understand basic anatomy. Bring a selection of teddy bears for the children to look at and discuss. You could ask the children to bring in their own teddy bear to make a collection for this project.

Resources

- Brown lightweight card
- Wool in various shades
- Buttons
- PVA glue
- Butterfly clips
- Red card

Approach

1. Hand out six pieces of pre-cut card rectangles.
2. Using one card for each body part of the teddy, draw a large oval for the body, a smaller circle for the head (including ears), two long 'sausage' shapes for the legs and two smaller 'sausage' shapes for the arms. Cut out as separate pieces and assemble on the table.
3. Using the different shades of brown wool, encourage the children to make teddy soft and furry by adding lots of texture. Pattern making with different tones also creates a nice effect.
4. Join teddy's body parts together with the butterfly clips (adult help needed here) allowing the limbs to move.
5. Glue the buttons onto the head to make the eyes and nose. Use the red card for the mouth, although buttons work equally well.

At the Pier

Resources

- Packaging – cardboard or plastic boxes and containers
- Selection of felt, fabric, tissue and coloured papers
- Scraps of wood, lolly sticks, modroc
- Wooden clothes pegs
- Acrylic paints
- PVA glue
- Pencils
- Scissors
- Masking tape
- Pipe cleaners
- Card
- Glue gun (adult use)

The history of the seaside is the history of leisure in Britain. Many activities associated with the seaside began during the Victorian era and remain the simple summer-time novelties enjoyed today. The aim of this project is for small groups to make a fairground ride or an attraction in a Victorian style that can be displayed on a pier that stretches into the sea. Prior to starting the project, discuss activities that children enjoy at the seaside.

The resources listed are suggestions, and although extensive rides can be made from whatever items are to hand, the list contains those resources used in the work illustrated. The idea is to be creative with what you have. Allow the children to use scrap materials in a resourceful way. Gather images such as a Ferris wheel, helter-skelter, and Punch and Judy for your starting point.

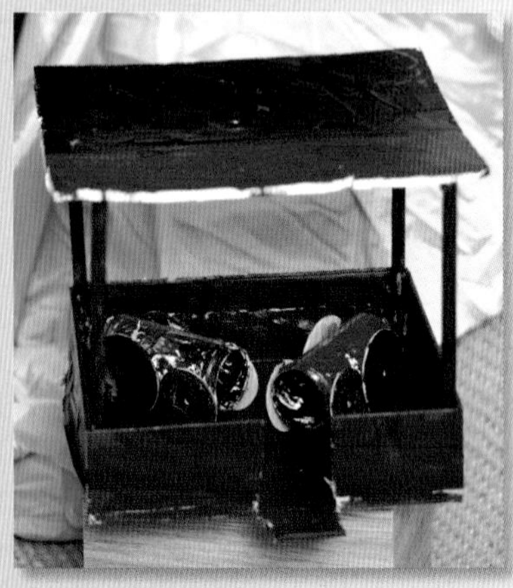

Approach

1. For the Punch and Judy theatre, stand a shoebox upright and cut out a window to create a theatre. Add the traditional red vertical stripes using paper strips.
2. Add a stand made from a piece of A4 card or wood, spread PVA glue over the surface and sprinkle with sand and shells if available.
3. Assemble hard surfaces securely with the glue gun.
4. For the puppets, use wooden clothes pegs and dress these using felt and fabric.
5. For the Ferris wheel, attach a circular form to a sturdy base, such as a block of wood, using the glue gun. Spokes, seats and figures on the ride can be made of card and pipe cleaners.
6. For the cup and saucers ride, cut up a biscuit tin plastic lining to form the cups and cover each one with modroc, sculpting a handle in the process. The saucers are old CDs.
7. For the dodgems, glue four sticks in each corner of a box to support a roof, and paint the interior of the box. To make the cars, use small containers and attach four disks to each side for the wheels.

Sunglasses

Designing a giant pair of sunglasses decorated with beach items is a fun way to bring many elements associated with the seaside together. Start by making a list with the children of things they might find at the beach, for example, ice cream, boats, fish, waves, sandcastles, bouncy balls, seaweed and crabs. The resources list is a suggestion, although most pieces can be made from whatever items are to hand.

Resources

- Cardboard
- Coloured acetate
- Coloured pencils
- Red and brown poster paint
- Sellotape
- PVA glue
- Coloured foam, fabric or felt
- Coloured paper
- Tissue paper

Approach

1. To create an over-sized pair of sunglasses, cut out two circle or square shapes from card. Cut out the centre part and attach the coloured acetate on the reverse side with sellotape. Put to one side.
2. To create the sunbathers, draw an outline on paper and colour using pencil. Cut out and stick on a price of fabric that becomes the towel.
3. To create the ice creams, fold a small card triangle into a cone shape and secure in place with sellotape. Line the cone with PVA glue, scrunch up tissue paper and tuck inside. Dribble on red or brown poster paint as flavoured sauces.
4. For the seaweed, twist tissue paper in different shades of green, glue on and allow to dangle from glasses frame.

5. For the fish and star fish, draw simple shapes on brightly coloured felt or paper and cut out. Glue on with PVA and twist and bend shapes a little to add movement to the fish.
6. To create the waves, cut wave patterns in different shades of blue and stick together in layers to illustrate the motion of the sea.

Night Fire Collages

The Great Fire of London started on 2 September and raged through the city until 5 September 1666. It began at the bakery of Thomas Farriner in Pudding Lane shortly after midnight, but the exact cause remains unknown. The fire swept through the city because winds fanned the flames and the houses were made of wood. It burned down 13,200 houses, and many were demolished in an effort to stop the fire's spread. The fire was put out once the strong east winds died down. No houses were to be made of wood thereafter, by order of King Charles II (1630–85).

Resources

- Black sugar paper size A3
- Orange, red and yellow paper
- Brown paper or Balsa wood
- Glue stick
- Scissors

Discuss the Great Fire of London with the children and encourage them to describe the atmosphere of that famous night in 1666.

Approach

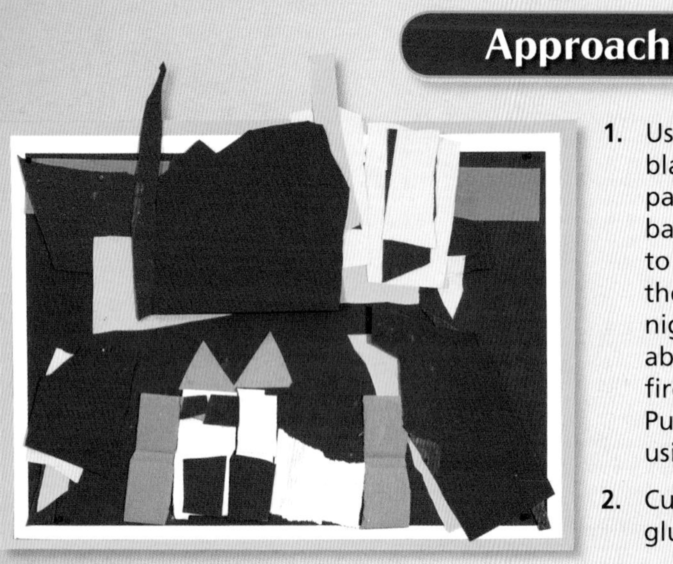

1. Use the black sugar paper as the background to represent the dark night. Talk about the fire in Pudding Lane and then ask the children to recreate the scene using the flame colours of yellow, orange and red.
2. Cutting the paper into flame shapes and sticking them with glue allows the children to play with scale.
3. Use the brown paper (or flakes of Balsa wood if available) for the houses.

The Streets are on Fire!

Resources

- Balsa wood, lolly sticks, scraps of small pieces of wood (without splinters)
- Clear plastic sheeting (e.g. from packaging)
- Stiff card approximately 20cm × 30cm
- Brown card (from cardboard box)
- Black sugar paper
- Masking tape
- Sellotape
- PVA glue
- Scissors

Look at the style of building from the seventeenth century, paying particular attention to the wooden frames, lattice windows and triangular roofs. There are two approaches to this project: each child makes their own model townscape of London, or makes a single building to contribute towards a whole-class model of London.

Approach

1. Use the stiff card as the base for the piece. Create the buildings using the pieces of wood and PVA glue.
2. Allow space in the buildings for the window(s) and cut the plastic sheet into pieces so that it can be inlayed into the building's frame.
3. To create a lattice window, cut thin strips of black paper and stick onto the clear plastic piece in a criss-cross fashion with the PVA glue. Attach the window on the inside using sellotape.
4. To make a roof, cut a rectangle from the brown cardboard, bending it into a sharp pointed roof and attach on the underside with tape.
5. The houses should look incomplete as they are supposed to be in a state of collapse! Gaps in the side, no roof or a hole in the roof will add to the authenticity.
6. For the flames, cut flame shapes and paint using red, yellow and orange paint.
7. When dry, place flames inside the house and position so that they are coming out of the roof and sides etc.
8. Use cotton wool or netting to create smoke, and attach with PVA glue.
9. For display purposes, assemble the children's work to recreate Pudding Lane. As an option, add a graphic-style backdrop showing a variety of buildings in silhouette.

The Pudding Lane Bakery

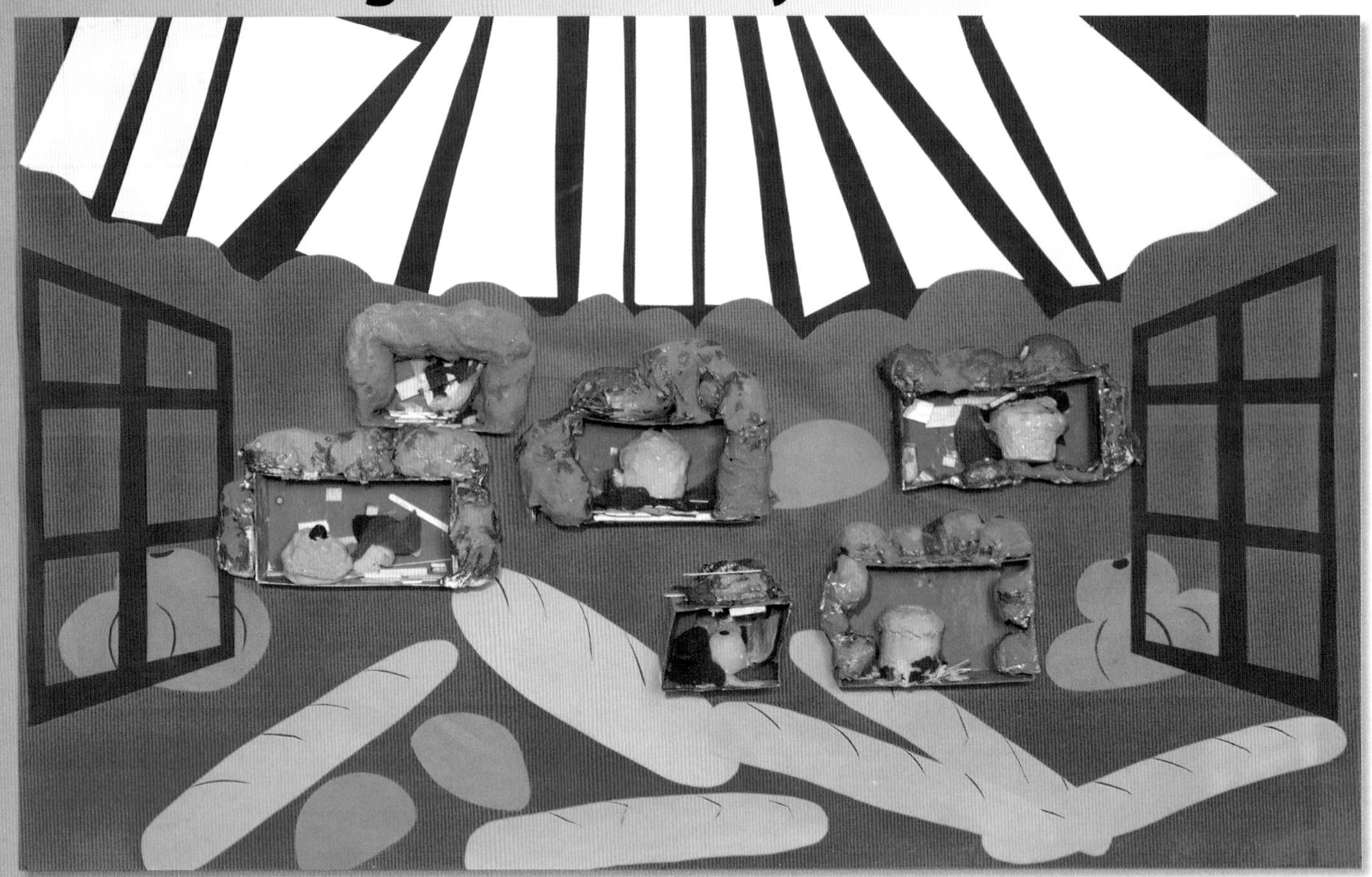

Resources

- Pictures of seventeenth-century domestic life and trading
- Shoeboxes
- Round container or pot
- Modroc
- Newspaper
- Poster paints

Pudding Lane is the name of the street where the Great Fire of London began. At that time most houses and shops were made of wood, so baking bread and pies must have been quite a dangerous job.

There was a great deal of mystery into how the fire started, but it was written that it was due to 'the hand of God, a great wind and a very dry season'. One source attributes the accident to a spark falling upon a bale of straw in the bakery of the Farriners, and many assume the spark to have come from an oven in the bakery. The ovens were made of stone and brick and every step was taken to be careful. Mr Farriner said that every night he made sure the oven door and windows were closed to stop a fire starting.

Approach

1. To create a pie, fill the container with newspaper pushed inside and pressed down.
2. Wrap the container in 2–3 layers of modroc, smoothing the surface as you go. For the top of the pie, add thicker amounts of modroc being careful not to flatten the newspaper underneath as this provides the bulky 'lid' of the pie. Allow to set hard.
3. Mix a 'biscuit' shade of paint to paint the pie. Add red for a cherry on top.
4. To create the oven, scrunch up newspaper and attach to the inside and outside of the shoebox with sellotape. Cover the entire model with modroc, smoothing it as you go. Paint when dry. Alternatively, use a stippled brush to create a textured surface on the oven.

Puppet Show

This project allows children to imagine life on the streets of London before the Great Fire began. By making individual houses that are then arranged together in a line, the bustling streets of London can come to life. The children can re-tell the story through the use of simple hand-held puppets. Begin the project by discussing life in London during this time. Talk about the sights, smells and general atmosphere of the city and compare it to life in a big city today. Listen to artists' impressions of life in London around the time of the Great Fire. For example, atmospheric readings from Samuel Pepys. Street names of the time included *Grub Streete, Gutter Lane, Milke Streete, Threadneedle Street,* and *Pie Corner.* These wonderful names give a vivid insight into the chaos of smells, textures and products of the city. People lived very close to one another and streets were narrow. There was poor sanitation and people would yell 'Watch out down below!' before emptying their waste from a bucket!

Resources

- Cardboard (packaging)
- Empty boxes
- Scissors
- Drawing pencil
- PVA glue
- Red, orange and yellow papers
- Masking tape
- Felt or paper
- Twine or wool
- Glue gun

Approach

1. Use an A4-sized piece of brown cardboard to create a house, ensuring that the thickness is suitable for cutting by hand. Cut out a triangular rooftop. Using a separate piece of card, cut out strips and rectangles to create tiles, wooden slats and window sills and glue into place.
2. Draw windows on the house, then these should be cut out by an adult.
3. Once dry, select a suitable-sized box and use the glue gun (adult use only) to attach it to the back of the house. This will enable the house to stand alone.
4. For each puppet, cut a small piece of card, draw the figure or animal (pigs, dogs etc.) and use felt, fabric, twine and wool to dress each one. Use paper to make the rising flames.
5. Use a thin length of stiff card to attach to the puppet as a handle.

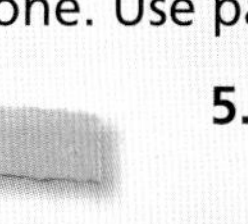

Egyptian Necklaces

Decoration and adornment were an important part of Egyptian society and acted as a status signifier. All the tombs show the wealthy and important wearing highly decorative and detailed forms of jewellery. Simpler versions were worn by people in authority such as soldiers and palace staff. The colours used in this project represent turquoise gemstones, coral and gold, the favoured materials of the pharaoh dynasties.

Approach

1. Using a circular template, draw a semi-circle on the black paper to the size of a necklace/collar and cut out.
2. Create a neck space by drawing a smaller semi-circle on the top edge of the collar (using a smaller diameter circle) and cutting out.
3. Use the large circle to draw a sequence of guidelines between the neck space and the outer edge of the collar.
4. Cut out pieces from the turquoise and orange paper, and decorate each line with a different colour.
5. Add the gold glitter to the collar.
6. Make the collar wearable by putting string on the two edges of the collar and tying together when on the wearer.

Resources

- Black sugar paper
- Turquoise paper
- Orange paper
- Gold glitter
- String
- Scissors

My Own Sarcophagus

This is a great project for helping to understand the concept of the 'Afterlife', which was so important to the Ancient Egyptians. It is also a good exercise in creating a contained little world in a variety of materials. Start by looking at the tale of Tutankhamun (1341BC–1322BC), his brief life, his death and the ritual involved in his preparation for the afterlife. Food, money and comfort can be made in miniature form and contained together in a sarcophagus.

Resources

- Shoebox × 1 per child
- Plastic bags or newspaper
- Sculpting wire
- Modroc
- Plasticine or clay
- Poster paint
- Coloured paper and card
- Sand (optional)
- Tissue paper

Approach

1. This project will take several sessions to complete, allowing for drying time and change of materials.
2. Begin by rolling the plastic bag or newspaper into a length that will fit inside the shoebox. Wrap with the sculpting wire and cover with three layers of modroc.
3. Paint the exterior of the box with brown paint (adding sand for texture). Using a different colour, each child should paint Tutankhamun's name in English on one side and in hieroglyphics on the other side.
4. Use gold and turquoise paper to decorate the lid like Tutankhamun's sarcophagus.

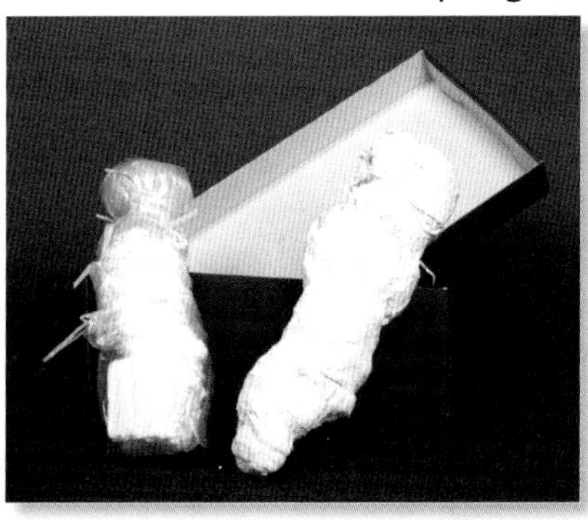

5. Line the interior of the box with tissue paper. Using the plasticine or clay, make a pot filled with items for the afterlife.
6. Complete the model by assembling all the parts. Display the lid and box on the wall using tacks through the back of the box.

Scarabs

A scarab beetle is the term used for a dung beetle. In Ancient Egypt they were thought to have special powers due to their habit of rolling a ball of dung uphill twice or three times their own size. The ball was seen as representing the sun, and worship of the sun was a big part of Egyptian life at the time. Small clay scarabs with writing on the underside were used in courts to seal judgements and important documents. In this project, the children make a scarab that has important secret information written on it in hieroglyphics.

Resources

- Red or grey clay
- Modelling tools
- PVA glue
- Poster or acrylic paints
- Thin brushes
- Hieroglyphic alphabet

Approach

1. Find pictures of a scarab, a dung beetle and an Egyptian seal as these are very useful references for detail and symmetry.
2. Knead the clay piece and model into an oval shape.
3. Using a point tipped modelling tool, carve a dividing line into the oval from top to bottom.
4. Continue drawing into the clay taking care to make the marks symmetrical on both sides.
5. On the underside, draw the hieroglyphics – ask the children to write their name or a secret message!
6. When the piece is completely dry (firing will make it much stronger), cover with a layer of PVA glue and allow to dry. This will create a barrier and prevent the paint from being absorbed.
7. Traditionally, scarabs were painted in turquoise, but a variety of colours also looks good when they are on display. Mix a colour with PVA glue to make the paint lustrous and shiny and paint on two coats.
8. Use a very fine brush to paint the carved markings and hieroglyphics with black paint.

Tutankhamun Sculpture

Begin by describing the construction of the pyramids in Ancient Egypt and the vast numbers of people and labour it involved. Look at the craftsmanship and materials used in making Tutankhamun's sarcophagus. Make a parallel with the task in hand, as this is a group project to construct a large-scale bust of the famous pharaoh.

Resources

- Empty cardboard packaging and shoeboxes
- Modroc or papier mâché
- Cardboard backing (e.g. a flattened cardboard box) approximately 1m × 75cm
- Poster paint
- Gold paint or paper

Approach

1. Organise the children into groups of 3–6 per table. Provide each group with a cardboard base laid on the table. Display a picture of Tutankhamun in a prominent position as a visual reference.
2. Ask the children to arrange the boxes in the shape of Tutankhamun and attach to the base using PVA glue.
3. Once dry, cover the boxes with modroc, draping it and moulding the features.
4. Cover the figure with a layer of watered-down PVA glue to create a non-porous barrier.
5. Once dry, paint the figure with blue poster paint mixed with PVA glue.
6. Use gold and coloured paint to add the remaining features and details.

Mummy Masks

Gather pictorial resources of death masks and coffins. Discuss the Ancient Egyptians' belief about the transformation from man to god state. Why were death masks so important? Can the children imagine what the person behind the mask was like?

Resources

- Pencil
- Card
- Coloured paper and metallic foils
- Skin tone crayons or coloured pencils
- Scissors
- Glue stick

Approach

1. Draw the basic shape of a head, complete with headdress, fake beard (if required) and collar. Once satisfied with the overall shape, carefully draw in the details of the face.
2. Lightly mark simple repeating patterns on the collar and headdress in pencil.
3. Using crayons, add skin tone and apply details to the face and beard (if it's a man!).
4. Cut the coloured paper and foil into strips and collage the headdress and collar, based on stripes and repeating patterns. Ensure no gaps are left between the glued pieces.
5. Once the collage is completed, carefully cut out the mask.
6. To create an Egyptian display in the classroom, gather motifs, materials and objects to display with the mummy masks. Use books and the internet to source images, and draw and cut out large-scale Egyptian objects using card.

Canopic Jars

Canopic jars were used to store the liver, lungs, intestines and stomach of a mummified body. The children can begin the project by carrying out research from books or the internet in order to make visual notes on which to base their own designs. This project can be completed in three sessions, allowing time for the clay to dry.

Approach

1. Split the clay into a large piece for the base and a smaller piece for the lid.
2. Roll both pieces into smooth balls. To create the jar, take the larger piece and form into a thumb pot, ensuring that the neck is not too wide. To maintain a cylindrical shape, periodically roll the jar on the clay board.
3. Using clay tools, carve hieroglyphics and motifs around the base of the jar.
4. Fashion the smaller ball into the head of a chosen character and use the tools to create detail.
5. Gently tap the head onto the clay board to create a flat base and trim with a clay knife to fit the rim of the jar.
6. Once the clay has dried, paint in authentic colours. Readymix paint dries quickly on clay, so fine details can be painted over the base colour.

Resources

- Photos of canopic jars
- Air drying clay
- Readymix paint (ochres, browns, blues, black and white)
- Gold metallic paint
- Range of brushes
- Palettes/water pots
- Clay boards/tools

Cartouches

A cartouche is an oval line enclosing a set of hieroglyphics that represent a person's name. A horizontal line at one end of the cartouche means that the hieroglyphics show the name of a king or queen.

The children can enjoy creating their own name in hieroglyphics, encircled within a cartouche. Examples of cartouches can be located in books and on websites about Egypt. Hieroglyphic alphabets can be found in most children's reference books on Egypt, or on the internet.

Resources

- Medium-density card for panel and frame
- Thin card for hieroglyphs
- Range of orange and yellow tissue paper
- Metallic gold paint
- Pencils
- Coloured pencils
- Ruler
- Fine black felt tip
- Watercolours
- Palettes/pots
- Fine brushes
- Scissors
- Craft knife and cutting board (for adult use only)

Approach

1. Draw a cartouche shape to form the back panel and cut out. A template may need to be provided. If the card is thick, an adult may need to use a craft knife.
2. To make the frame, draw around the cartouche to replicate the shape and cut out.
3. Cut out the middle to form the inner edge of the frame.
4. Lay the frame to one side and tear the yellow and orange tissue paper into small pieces.
5. Stick the tissue paper randomly onto the back panel to create an overlapping mosaic effect.
6. Paint the frame with gold metallic paint and leave to dry.
7. Carefully write a name in hieroglyphics onto the card. Make it large enough to be easily cut out.
8. Colour the hieroglyphics by either painting with fine brushes or using coloured pencils.
9. Cut out the hieroglyphics and stick vertically onto the cartouche.
10. Stick the frame onto the base and decorate in black pen with a range of hieroglyphics.

Egyptian Paintings

The focus of this project is to tell a story through painting, very much like the way tomb paintings depicted the life events of the deceased. The children can base the visual stories on themselves, or on paintings they have researched. The project is particularly suitable for work in small groups as it can encourage communication skills and collaboration.

There is a wealth of resources on the internet and in books which show images of Egyptian tomb paintings.

Resources

- Pencil
- Scrap paper for practising ideas
- Good quality card, pre-marked with a gird of equal sections
- Watercolours
- Palettes/water pots
- Range of brushes
- Scissors

Approach

1. Ask the children to work out a design on scrap paper.
2. Transfer the design onto the grid of the card. Each child needs to take responsibility for one or two sections of the gird.
3. Carefully cut out the card into the separate pieces and each child paints their own section, selecting appropriate brushes for backgrounds and fine detail. The children need to work collaboratively with their group to ensure colour matching; however, the appeal of these paintings are the variations in style and tone.
4. Once the paintings are dried, 'jigsaw' them back together to create a whole image.

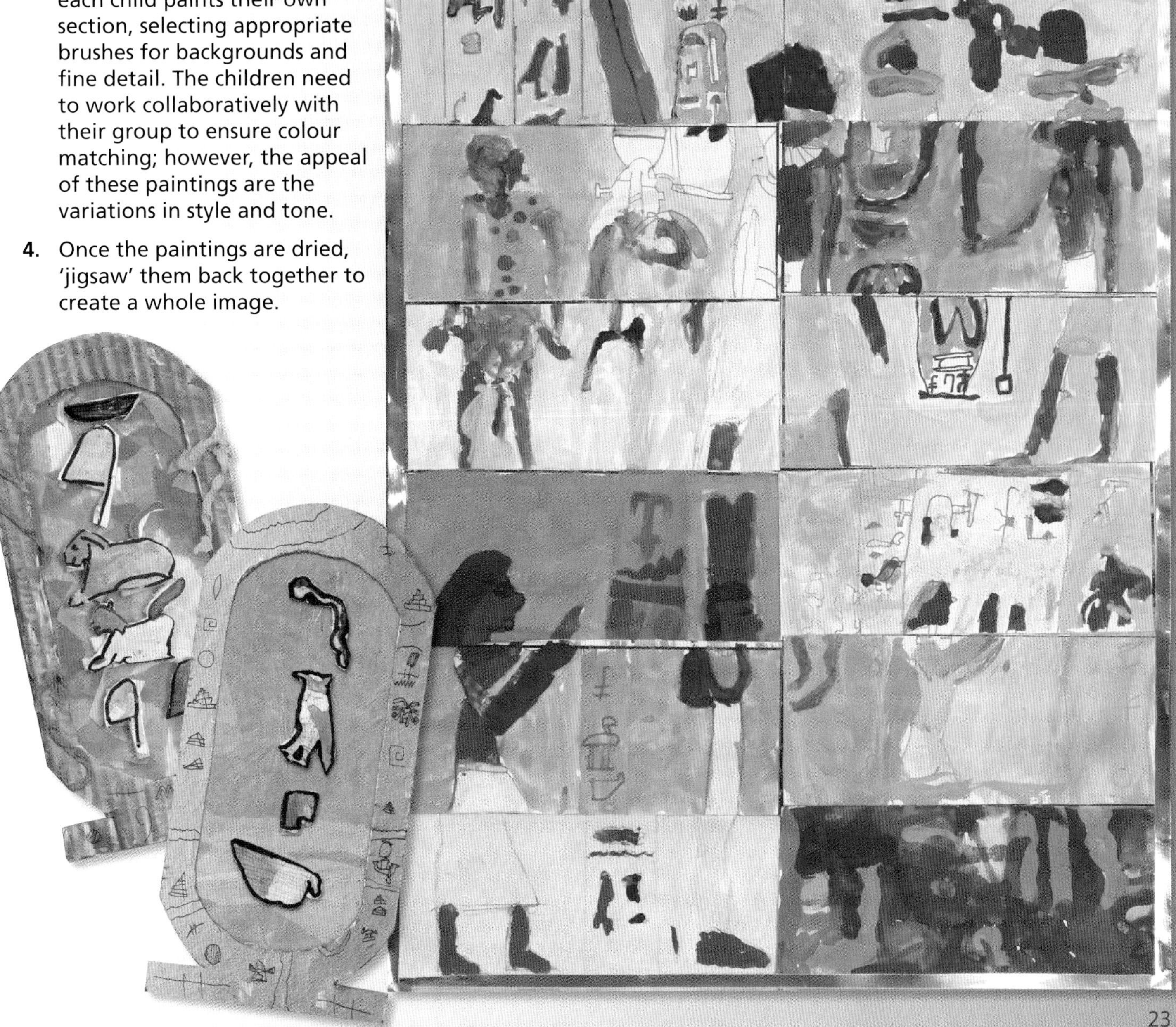

A Show at the Amphitheatre

It is said that theatre was born in the Greek amphitheatre. The grand, large-scale, circular, open-air buildings were a place of entertainment for the Ancient Greeks, who would go there to watch plays and listen to political ideas. They were a place of gathering and a place of spectacle. The circular design 'in the round' meant that everyone had a good view of the stage. Begin the project by looking at images of existing amphitheatres. You can find these in travel brochures, and most will be in a state of ruin. Children's history books are illustrated with re-enactments of life in Ancient Greece. Compare the two, and discuss what kind of arenas we use today to watch football, the cinema, concerts etc.

Resources

- Flexible card
- Ruler
- Drawing pencil
- Sellotape
- PVA glue
- Corrugated paper
- Pale grey poster paint
- Circles in two sizes – large and smaller
- Cartridge paper
- Colour pencils
- Modroc
- Camera

Approach

1. To form the base for the ampitheatre seating, create a ring by first drawing a large circle on the card and then drawing a smaller circle placed in the centre of the larger one. Position the smaller circle as centrally as possible, keeping an equal measurement between both circles all around the ring.
2. Cut out the outer circle and cut a line through the ring towards the inner circle. Cut out the inner circle then over lap the ring to create a cone shape. Secure in place using sellotape.
3. Cut a length of corrugated paper to fit the height of the cone to create the outer wall. Secure to the upper edge of the cone with sellotape. Cut away a front section taking care that the circular structure stays in place.
4. Use thin strips of the corrugated paper to create the amphitheatre seating. Cover structure with a layer of modroc to create a stone-like texture. Once dry, dab on grey paint using a piece of fabric or tissue to create a mottled effect.
5. For the audience, use flexible card to draw groups of people in Ancient Greek attire. Colour in using coloured pencil. Bend the figures at the knees and seat using PVA glue to secure in the amphitheatre.
6. For the actors, assemble small groups of children and encourage them to act out and stage a scene from a Greek myth. Photograph, print, mount on card and place on the stage. Also try adding modroc clothes to the photographs.

Greek Pottery

Images of Greek terracotta pottery emblazoned with gods and goddesses provide an inspiring starting point for children to research Greek mythology. Children should be encouraged to depict their favourite myth on their own vase, or provide a more contemporary version based on themselves and their hobbies. It is important for the children to practise drawing some initial ideas first.

Resources

- Balloons
- Newspaper
- PVA glue (equally mixed with water)
- Spreaders
- Scissors
- Masking tape
- Acrylic paint – white, black, ochre, brown, orange and black
- Range of brushes
- Palettes

Approach

1. Blow up a balloon and methodically cover with thin strips of newspaper, applying a generous amount of PVA glue mixture. Repeat until at least four layers have been applied. Ensure that there are no gaps, that the layers are distributed evenly and that the top layer has been smoothed down. Leave to dry for three days.
2. Once dry, gently cut into the tied end of the covered balloon to create an aperture that will form the rim of the vase. Ensure that the rim is evenly cut to the desired circumference. Pull out the deflated balloon.
3. To create a stable base, affix a ring of rolled up newspaper around the base of the vase with masking tape.
4. Build up another four layers of papier mâché around the join of the base and cover all exposed strips of masking tape. Leave to dry for another three days.
5. Using acrylic paint, apply a base coat of a terracotta colour to both the inside and the outside of the vase.
6. Once dry, gently draw the chosen figurative design around the pot. Repeating patterns and borders look particularly effective around the rim or the base.
7. Once satisfied with the drawing, proceed to paint the motifs using a fine brush and authentic colours.

Clay Greek Temples

Resources

- Pencils/paper for initial designs
- Rule
- Air drying clay
- A4 white paper or card for the roof
- Range of clay tools
- Rolling pin
- Clay board
- Water pots
- White paint
- Brushes
- Palettes
- Aprons

This project focuses on the pillars or columns used in Ancient Greek architecture and the pediment, which often contained sculptures depicting scenes from mythology. Make sketches of the different styles. The project will take 2–4 sessions. If the clay work takes longer, it is important to store the models in airtight polythene.

Approach

1. Using their sketches or reference material, the children should design a temple incorporating a pediment and column style of their choice.
2. To make the temple base, roll a piece of clay to about 1cm thickness and cut out a rectangle or square. Using a rule to mark out and cut the base will ensure a uniform shape. Once made, cover and put aside.
3. Repeat the above process to make the plinths and tops for the columns. For the plinths, cut out small cubes of equal size (about 2cm). For the tops (if required), make thinner and slightly wider versions. Once made, cover and put aside.
4. To make the columns, roll a large piece of clay into a smooth ball. Roll the ball into a 'sausage' shape of equal thickness. This can be tricky for young children and is best done on a clay board. Start in the middle of the cylinder and the clay will grow outwards. It is important to keep the hands moving along the cylinder, focusing on any uneven areas, and to stop when the cylinder is about 1.5cm, or no thicker than the width of the column bases. Cut the cylinder into equal lengths (not too long) to form the columns. Roll extra cylinders if needed.
5. Using slip (a 'glue' mixture of clay and water), score the raw edges and stick the small cube plinths onto the base to match the design. Carefully stick the columns onto these, ensuring they remain parallel to each other. Finally, stick the tops on the pillars very carefully. At this stage some children prefer to make scrolls in ionic features for the top of their columns. Small cylinders can be rolled and curled but use slip in the sticking process. Set the clay model aside for at least four days to dry thoroughly.
6. Once dry, paint all the clay with white poster paint. The temples are quite delicate, but any disasters can be fixed with PVA glue!
7. For the roof and pediment, make a card prism net to the same dimensions as the base. On a triangle face of the net that will form the pediment, draw a 'sculpture relief' depicting a mythological scene. Stick the net together with stronger PVA and glue on top of the clay temple.

Building a Temple

A good introduction to this activity is to retell a Greek myth. Theseus and the minatour is a popular tale, as are tales of the Greek gods who use their powers to shape the destiny of others (can be found on internet or children's books). The temples were highly sacred buildings and not entered by anyone other than priests. They were to house the gods and cult figures that people looked up to.

Resources

- Shoeboxes
- White acrylic paint
- Wooden clothes pegs × 6 or 8 per temple
- Modroc
- Wine bottle corks
- Ruler
- Drawing pencil
- White flexible card
- Coloured paper
- Glue gun (adult use)
- PVA glue

Approach

1. Use a white shoebox or paint the outside of a shoebox or its lid. Use one or the other and turn it upside down to form the base of the temple.
2. Measure a piece of card equal to the length and width of the temple base, with two additional rectangles of the same measurement on either side. Fold along the two lines to create a triangular roof and stick together with sellotape. Put to one side.
3. Create the columns by attaching a peg to a cork with masking tape. Cover each peg with modroc, sculpting and building up each figure and its features to included toga dress, a long beard and so on. Ensure that all 6 or 8 columns are the same height. Put to one side and allow to dry out fully.
4. Add stairs to the two sides of the temple base using white paper or card folded back and forth. Attach using PVA glue.
5. Create a mosaic pattern on the floor of the temple using small squares of cut coloured paper.
6. Space the columns equally apart and use the glue gun (adult use) to glue the columns upright onto the temple base. Once they are stable, put a drop of hot glue onto the head of each statue and lower on the temple roof.

Roman Oil Lamps

There is a wealth of resources in books, museums and on the internet on Roman art and artefacts. These oil lamps are easy to make and great fun to decorate. The quirkiness and individuality of each lamp adds to the impression that they are 'ancient' and look great displayed as excavated objects! This project can be completed in one session.

Resources

- Terracotta clay
- Clay boards
- Pot of water
- Cutting tools
- Rolling pin
- Straws/dowelling/pencils/ forks for indenting patterns

Approach

1. View examples of Roman oil lamps, focusing on the patterns and the reason for the two holes in the lid.
2. To make the bottom of the lamp, roll a piece of clay the size of a tennis ball into a smooth ball. Ensure children use the heel of their hands as opposed to their fingers and keep turning the clay to create an even finish.
3. Once smooth, gently insert the handle of the rolling pin into the ball of clay and twist gently to form a hollow.
4. Holding the ball carefully with one hand, insert the thumb into the hole and gently pinch the sides of what now looks like a bowl. Rotate constantly in the palm of the hand so that the thickness of the sides remains even. The aperture in the bowl will slowly expand. Take care not to make the sides too thin. Once satisfied with the 'bowl', smooth the exterior using a small amount of water if necessary.
5. Slam the bowl firmly once onto the clay board to create a flat base.
6. To create the lid, take a small piece of clay and roll into a pancake, no thicker than 1cm. Place the bowl upside down onto the pancake to form a template. Cut around the bowl and then remove it leaving a small circle for the lid.
7. Using a clay knife, carefully score around the rim of the bowl to create a rough edge. Do the same to the edge of the lid where the clay is to be joined.
8. Smear water onto the rim of the bowl and the place the lid firmly on top. Cut off any excess flap and join and smooth the seam.
9. To create the teardrop shape of the lamp, hold it between two hands and gently squeeze one end until it narrows into the desired shape.
10. Using the knife, cut a small hole in the lid to create an oil aperture and use the dowelling or a pencil to create the hole for the wick.
11. Finally, use the implements to carve or indent repeating patterns onto the oil lamp.

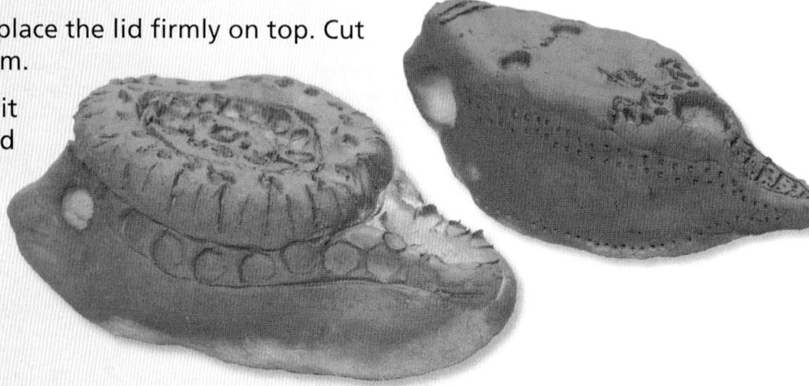

Roman Mosaics

Mosaics took a long time to create as each one was made up of small pieces of stone or ceramic. They were very expensive to make, so only the wealthy and important people had them in their houses. The designs often showed pictures of Roman gods, gladiator battles and also animals. There are places in Britain where Roman mosaics can be seen, such as the British Museum in central London. To see mosaics in their original setting, visit Lullingstone Roman Villa in Kent, or Bignor Roman Villa in West Sussex (many are in the south of England – research the internet to find out if there are any Roman remains in your area).

This activity focuses on the effectiveness of repetition of pattern and colour.

Resources

- Polystyrene tiles (educational art suppliers stock the specialised smooth textured variety)
- Pencils
- PVA glue
- Ready-mix poster paint
- Water pots
- Scissors
- Spreaders
- Range of brushes
- Palettes

Approach

1. Ask children to work out a design for their mosaic. It is important to keep the design really simple, as it may be hard to replicate complex designs in squares of polystyrene.
2. Cut numerous, equally sized squares of polystyrene ready to stick onto the base square.
3. Lightly draw the chosen design onto the base tile as a guide, and then use the PVA glue to stick on the pieces to produce the required pattern. Borders look particularly effective.
4. Once the base tile is dry, paint the mosaic, treating each square individually. Focus on variations of tone and repeating patterns for a really authentic look.

Roman People

Look at pictures of Roman mosaics that show people fighting in battle and discuss their uniform. Does the 'skirt' that men wear look practical? Do you think the helmet is metal? And therefore heavy? Other mosaics show people relaxing at the communal baths wearing tunics. Both images reflect the lifestyle of the Romans. Excerpts from films can also show vividly how the Romans lived and what they wore.

Resources

- Old-fashioned clothes pegs
- Ready-mix paint (yellow ochre, brown, white and red) to create flesh tones
- Range of brushes
- Palettes
- Water pots
- Wool for hair
- Pipe cleaners
- Fabric for togas, dresses etc.
- Red material for capes
- Tin foil
- Card
- Red feathers
- Beads
- PVA glue

Approach

1. Paint the top third of the peg in appropriate flesh tone. Once dry, paint facial features.
2. Wrap a pipe cleaner around the 'neck' of the peg to form arms.
3. Cut fabric into a rectangle and fold in half. Cut a small hole for the neck and place onto the doll to form a tunic. Snip the rectangle under both the arms and glue the sides to form sleeves.
4. Wrap wool around the waist to make a belt. Plaited ones look great.
5. If the doll is a gladiator, cut a piece of red fabric and wrap around the neck to form a cape. Leather 'skirts' for the gladiators can be made by fringing a rectangular piece of fabric and wrapping it around the figure.
6. To make hair, cut strands of wool and glue onto the head. Once dry, this can be cut into the desired style. If the doll is a goddess, beads can be glued into her hair.
7. To make a Roman helmet, mould tin foil into a helmet shape and insert a feather into the top to create a plume. Trim the feather to the right proportions. Glue the helmet into place onto the head.
8. Roman swords can be moulded out of tin foil. Roman rectangular shields are made by cutting card into shape and covering with foil. Using a sharp pencil, patterns can be engraved onto the foil.

Roman Standards

A Roman Standard is a flag that announces who a group are. They were used by the Roman army and carried at the front of each legion (group of soldiers). The army was so big that it was necessary to label each legion, and the Standard usually showed the legion's name and its number written in Roman numerals.

The internet provides a rich reference source of examples of Roman standards. Use these for a discussion about what the children would put on their own standard. What elements of their own history, hobbies or interests would they depict? How could they ensure that it would be seen from a distance? The children could share various ideas and make thumbnail sketches of different variations. Which colours would they choose? Would they incorporate writing or initials?

Children enjoy the versatility of working in both 2-D and 3-D in paper. It encourages the development of fine motor skills and a sense of design. Pleasing results can be obtained without the 'pressure' of drawing accurately through the innovative use of colour and shape.

Resources

- Short dowelling
- A5 card in various colours
- Range of coloured card and paper for collage
- Foil
- Scissors
- Glue sticks
- Adhesive tape

Approach

1. The children decide upon a design for their standard and then select an A5 card in the colour of their choice to form the background for the standard. Draw and cut out the elements needed for the standard. Lay them on the card (without sticking) and adjust their positions until the layout is satisfactory.
2. When the elements are correctly positioned, stick them onto the card. The children may then wish to embellish their designs with patterns or borders in contrasting or complementing colours.
3. Using the adhesive tape, secure the standard onto the top of the dowelling.
4. Make a crest for the standard to complement the theme in whichever method the children choose. Origami shapes, card cut-outs or motifs are popular choices.

Roman Sandals

Resources

- Range of card for straps and soles
- Split pins
- Coloured paper for decoration
- Scissors
- Glue sticks

Look at the design of Roman sandals in books or on the internet. Encourage children to make sketches of their own designs. How would they ensure that their sandals would not slip off their feet? What kind of person are they designing their sandal for? Gladiator? Slave? Citizen? Would decoration be appropriate?

Approach

1. Ask the children to draw around their bare feet on a piece of card. They do not need to draw around each of the toes. They need to trace two outlines for each foot – one for the bottom sole and one for an inner sole.
2. To make the bottom soles, select a pair of foot outlines and cut around the shapes about 5mm outside the original drawing. Explain that all shoes and sandals need to be made slightly bigger than the feet to ensure easy fit and comfort.
3. Using their sketches as reference, select more card and cut out the appropriate number of straps for each sandal. Care needs to be taken that the straps are long enough for the job they need to do.
4. Attach the straps to the top of the sole following their own design.
5. Cut out the remaining two outlines that form the inner sole. This time cut exactly along the line. Place the inner soles over the bottom soles. These will hide the stuck ends of the straps and give a neat finish.
6. Decorate the straps with split pins that will look very similar to rivets. If desired, the children can decorate the sandals in any method they choose.

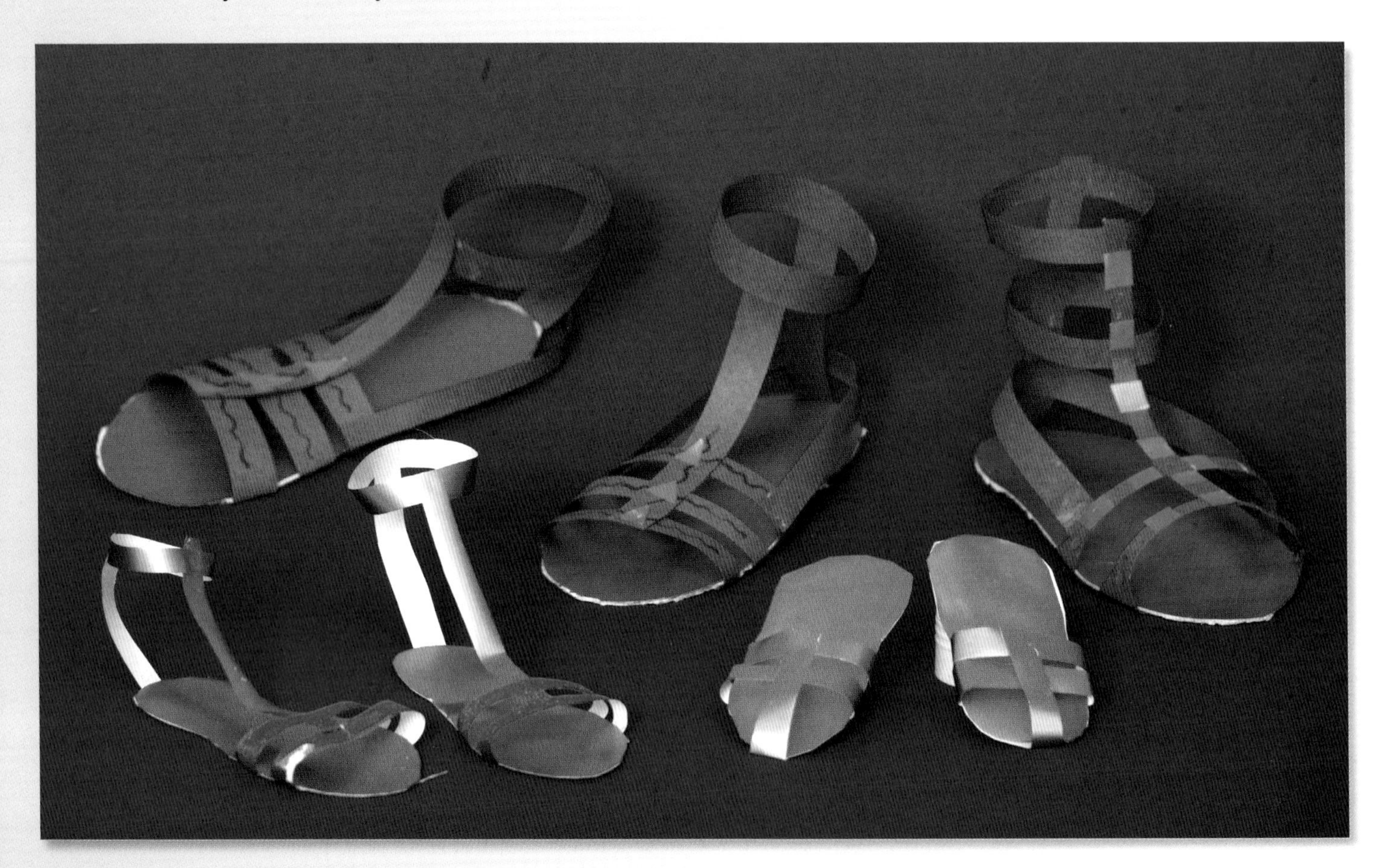

Living in Ancient Britain

Resources

- Large paper cup or light card cone shape with tip removed
- String, twine, wool, leather strips
- PVA glue
- Cardboard rectangle approx 20 x 25cm
- Green paper
- Scissors
- Plasticine
- Photos of children – optional

Look at pictures of houses built by the Saxons, Celts and Vikings. A common factor of the buildings is the materials used – wattle and daub, and thatched pointed roofs. In a discussion, create a picture of what life would have been like. Encourage the children to visualise a place without the buildings we see today – wide open fields and small dwellings with cattle and crops.

Approach

1. To make a house from a paper cup, turn the cup upside down and cut a small doorway. To make from card, roll the card into a cone shape, secure with sellotape and cut off the tip to size.
2. Starting from the bottom of the cup, cover the lower half with PVA glue and wrap with twine, string or leather strips. Continue the process upwards completely covering the house. Trim the string covering the doorway to reveal the doorway again.
3. For a pointed roof, cut out a circle approx 20cm in diameter. Cut from the edge to the centre point, fold round to make a cone and attach to the house. For a two-sided roof, bend in half a 20 x 10cm piece of card and attach to the house with sellotape. Decorate using the string or paper to make a thatched-effect roof.
4. Using PVA glue, cover the lower rim of the house to place on the cardboard strip and allow to dry.
5. Using the green paper, cut vertical lines to fray the paper, bend to look like grass and stick to the cardboard. Make vegetables from the plasticine to put growing outside the house.
6. Finally, ask each child to describe what they would be doing if they lived in their house – planting or picking vegetables, feeding chickens etc. Photograph them enacting their pose and add the photo to the home.

Viking Helmets

The Vikings arrived in Britain during the eighth to eleventh century. Children love Viking culture and mythology. Their armour and weaponry particularly seem to fascinate all ages. It is debatable whether horned helmets 'en masse' really existed; however, for the sake of artistic licence, they have been included in this topic. The shields are mainly of a circular design, embellished with simple patterns or runic lettering. Examples of helmets, shields and the runic alphabet can be located on the internet or in specialist books.

Resources

- Contour wire mesh
- Polythene sheeting (for the floor)
- Old bucket or bowl
- Ready-mix paint in metallic pewter, ochre, brown and black
- Palettes
- Modroc
- Disposable gloves (modroc can irritate sensitive skin)
- Scissors
- Paint pots
- Range of brushes

Approach

1. For the helmet, cut a circle of contour mesh with scissors to approximately double the width of the child's head. This may have to be done by an adult as the edges are quite sharp. Cut a slit from the edge to the middle point of the circle and manipulate the wire to form a coned helmet.
2. Mould two more pieces of wire to make two horns. Cut two slits into the coned helmet and position the horns, manipulating the wire to secure them. Fold over any raw edges.
3. Wet a modroc strip and carefully lay over the contour wire helmet. Repeat until the whole helmet is covered. Smooth any bumps with wet hands.
4. Once dry, paint the helmet in a mixture of metallic paint or brown to depict leather. Paint the horns white to look like bone.

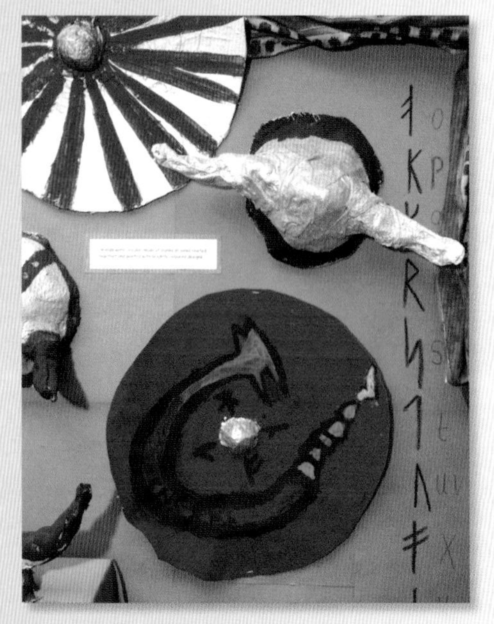

Shields

Approach

1. For the shield, cut the card into a circle. If a craft knife is used for this, ensure that an adult uses it.
2. Cover the circle with papier mâché, building up raised areas in the middle or on the rim of the shield.
3. Once dry, paint to the specified design. Simple god effigies or runic letters look authentic.
4. A strip of cardboard can be attached to the back of the shield so it can be held.

Resources

- Thick card
- Craft knife (for adult use only)
- PVA glue and water mixture
- Newspaper
- Ready-mix paint
- Palettes
- Range of brushes

Queen Victoria Portrait

As a monarch who reigned for nearly a century, Queen Victoria's image has become iconic. To explore this aspect, look at the work of artist Andy Warhol (1928–87), who was fascinated by the iconic imagery of America (Disney, Coca-Cola, Marilyn Monroe etc.). His use of very bright colours also brings something novel to the Victorian era, which is normally pictured in black and white or sepia. As a starting point, look at photographs of Queen Victoria.

Resources

- Portrait of Queen Victoria size A2
- Card board approx size A2
- Pencil
- Poly block
- Scissors
- PVA glue
- Printing inks or acrylic paint in a variety of colours
- A2 sheets of paper in black, white and a variety of bright colours
- Printing rollers
- Plastic tray or sheet
- Colour wheel diagram (can be made from paint colour strips)

Approach

1. Draw a picture of Queen Victoria on the board. Draw particular attention to the main features of her portrait: the diagonal sash, the crown, proportion of the picture taken up by her head and shoulders etc.
2. Cut small pieces of the poly block sheet to fill in the picture and stick on with generous amounts of PVA.
3. In preparation for the colour work, it is worthwhile looking at colour theory. Those colours that are opposite each other on the wheel will be very vibrant together. The same is true of light and dark highlighting. Encourage the children to use this system when selecting the colour of the paper and paint they work with.
4. Allow for 3–5 prints to be produced, each time changing the colour combination between the paint and paper. Try to clean the print block using tissue paper, though if other colours appear, they will enhance the effect.
5. Allow first series of prints to dry completely, then use new colours to create an overlay of new colour.

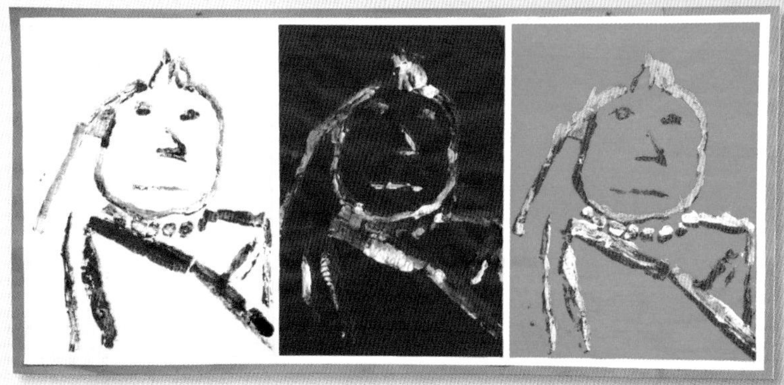

Story Boxes

For this project, focus on either Mary Seacole (1805–81) or Florence Nightingale (1820–1910) or compare the two. Mary Seacole's story is one of courage, resourcefulness and determination. She travelled to the Crimea at her own expense and set up the 'British Hotel' near the battlefield at Balaclava. Her passion for helping the wounded took her onto the battlefield, where she risked her life tending soldiers amidst cannon fire. This project is an ideal way of understanding the different and dangerous environments she worked in.

Florence Nightingale's reform of British military hospitals in Turkey gives an insight into how her dedication and passion influenced the standard of care in hospitals today. Together with the story of Mary Seacole, children can explore how determination and self-belief can make a difference under difficult circumstances. Using the boxes for role play is an excellent starting point for paired discussion and writing projects.

Resources

- Shoeboxes
- Ready-mix poster paint
- Range of brushes
- Palettes
- Water pots
- Scissors
- Range of card
- Green tissue paper
- Fabric for collage
- Coloured pencils
- Glue sticks
- Tin foil

Approach

1. For Mary Seacole, use visual aids to help discuss the battlefield environment where Mary tended the wounded.
2. Cut two vertical seams at the front of the shoebox to create a flap. Paint a landscape inside the box, complete with horizon line and sky, extending to the front flap. Make trees and bushes by scrunching tissue paper or by constructing in card. To construct cannons,roll, cut and paint card accordingly. Place within the diorama.

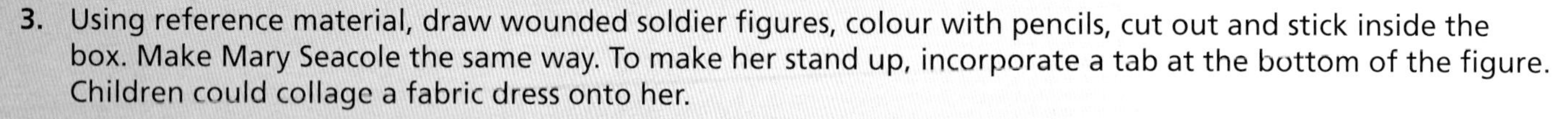

3. Using reference material, draw wounded soldier figures, colour with pencils, cut out and stick inside the box. Make Mary Seacole the same way. To make her stand up, incorporate a tab at the bottom of the figure. Children could collage a fabric dress onto her.
4. Decorate the outside of the box and lid as appropriate.
5. For Florence Nightingale, use visual resources to help discuss the differences between Florence's hospitals and those of today.
6. Cut two vertical seams at the front of the shoebox to create a flap. Cut windows into the sides of the box. Paint the interior with a wooden floor and plain white walls.
7. To make the beds, cut small rectangles of card with flaps on each corner of the same length. When folded, these 'legs' form the base of a bed.

8. To make cupboards, fold a rectangle of card into thirds. Fold the two outer flaps inwards to create a 3-D shape. For the cupboard shelves, cut slits symmetrically at either end of the flaps and slot narrow rectangles of card between themelves.
9. Mould buckets and bowls out of tin foil. Make blankets, curtains, bandages and pillows from scrap collage fabric.
10. For the wounded soldiers, draw and cut out card figures and colour with pencils. Make Florence the same way. To make her stand up, incorporate a flap at the bottom of the figure.
11. Arrange and glue in furniture and figures as required.
12. Paint the outside of the box and lid as appropriate.

William Morris

William Morris (1834–96) was an artist, writer and social thinker. Images of his wallpaper and tapestry designs can be found in art books and on the internet, and his fabrics are sold by Liberty Stores, London. Emphasise the use of symmetry in his work and his love of nature. The palette is very subtle and in preparation for the activity, explain harmony and opposite colour schemes with use of a colour wheel. You can make a colour wheel by collecting colour sample sheets from DIY and paint stores.

Resources

- Real or artificial plants or flowers
- A2 sugar paper
- Drawing pencil
- Chalk pastels
- Water colours

Approach

1. Begin with a discussion about the form of each plant. Draw particular attention to the shape and size of the leaves and petals.
2. In preparation for the drawing, encourage the children to enlarge the plant they are drawing and to repeat the motif in a symmetrical way utilising the whole sheet of paper.
3. Select three harmonious colours on the colour wheel and use these to paint the design.
4. Once dry, use the colour pastels to add depth and texture to the work.

Crystal Palace and the Great Exhibition

In 1851, Queen Victoria and her husband, Prince Albert, decided to hold a grand exhibition to display all the latest craft and technology being pioneered in Britain at the time. The building housing the Great Exhibition, as it was called, was Crystal Palace and was a revolutionary in architectural terms as it was made completely of glass. The building burnt down years later, but pictures of Crystal Palace can be found on the internet. This project can be adapted for a focus on Victorian railway stations or railway arches. Begin with a discussion about the shapes that appear in the design of the building – arch, semi-circle, rectangle, vertical and horizontal lines.

Resources

- Black paper
- White paper
- Silver paper or card
- Polystyrene chunks or similar
- Glue stick
- Scissors
- Ruler
- Compass or round object
- Cutting knife (adult use only)
- Cutting mat (adult use only)

Approach

1. Using the cutting knife, cutting mat and ruler, cut the length of an A3 piece of black paper (or white if in reverse) into strips approximately 0.5cm wide.
2. Make the picture using these lengths of paper cut to size. Distribute the lengths of paper, and encourage the children to recreate the horizontal and vertical lines that make up the steel-framed structure of the building.

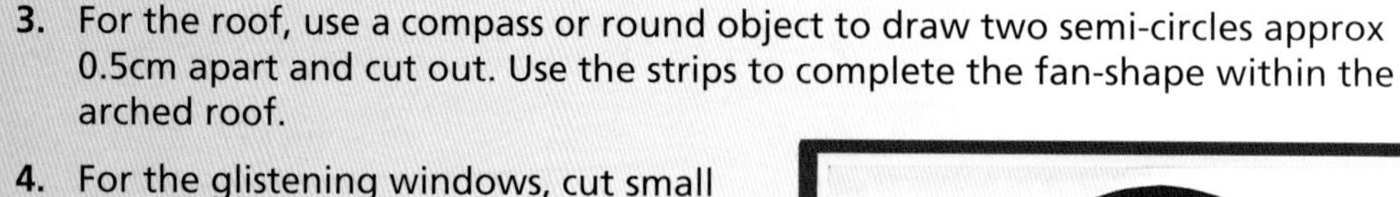

3. For the roof, use a compass or round object to draw two semi-circles approx 0.5cm apart and cut out. Use the strips to complete the fan-shape within the arched roof.
4. For the glistening windows, cut small silver squares and place within the window frames. Add a 3-D effect by sticking down a small piece of polystyrene or similar and then gluing a silver square on top.

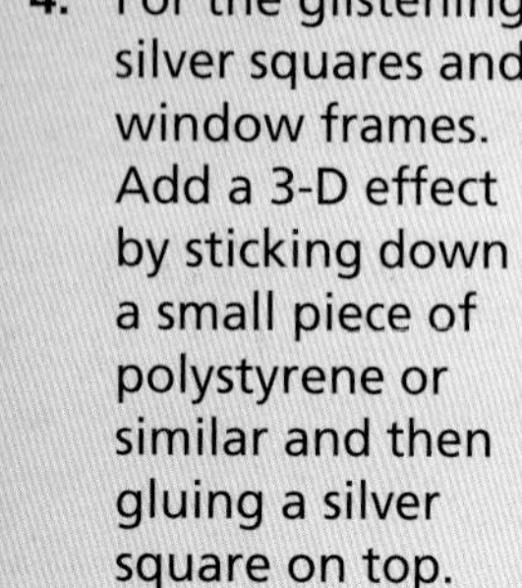

Cog Montage

This project ties in well with the Industrial Revolution (c.1760–c.1830). The idea is to produce a class 'machine' using the media of chalk pastels and paint. It also introduces the difficult subject of drawing circles.

It is hard to bring examples of the inner workings of machines into school, especially cogs. There may be opportunities for the children to see the inner workings of an old clock or watch or a plastic cog construction toy from early years departments. Alternatively, photographic examples can be found on the internet.

As a starting point, discuss with the children how they think one cog could set another in motion. Notice how the cogs need to touch and interlock in a ratchet system. A fun activity is to create a human spinning cog formation, with children stretching out their arms and interacting with each other. Good supervision is needed to prevent injury!

As a 5 minute warm-up exercise, ask the children to draw circles in freehand in as many varying sizes as they can on one sheet of paper. Do they find the task easier after a few minutes? Can they make the perfect circle?

Resources

- Black sugar paper cut into wide strips
- Chalk pastels in browns, oranges, reds, yellows and whites
- Pencils
- Pairs of compasses
- Light coloured card
- Metallic paint
- Scissors
- Glue sticks
- Adhesive putty

Approach

1. Lightly draw in pencil circles of different sizes, touching and overlapping each other. Draw freehand or use a pair of compasses if preferred.
2. Once the arrangement is satisfactory, children should redraw over the outlines in a coloured chalk of their choice. Using one finger, gently smudge and blur the chalk outline, which thickens it and gives the illusion of movement. Draw the cog's teeth over the top.
3. If desired, drag white chalk over areas of the cog to produce a metallic reflective effect or 'rim light' the edges of the teeth with white or yellow highlights. When the drawings are finished, stick them together on large sheets of sugar paper to create one giant cog machine.
4. More cogs can be made by painting them onto light coloured card with metallic paint. Once dry, cut these out carefully and position them over the class montage with adhesive putty. This raises them off the drawing to produce a 3-D effect.

School Life

Schooling for Britain's children in the Victorian era was a new initiative; it was very strict and the surroundings were very basic. As most children lived in absolute poverty, they were expected to work in harsh conditions when not at school. To help children make a comparison between then and now, begin by asking them to describe their school environment with particular attention to materials (plastic chairs, computers etc.). Look at photographs of Victorian schools. By making a wooden chair and dressing as a Victorian child, they can gain a glimpse into the past.

Approach

1. To create the chair, cut a rectangle out of card. At a point 20cm along the long side, draw a line across (adult only) and bend into a seated position.
2. Spread PVA glue on the bottom side of four paper cups and position one half of the cardboard piece on to them. Allow to dry.
3. To keep the back of the chair upright, use the glue gun to attach a lolly stick vertically to the reverse side of the chair and to a chair leg.
4. Mix water with some PVA glue into a milky fluid. Dip in the tissue paper and apply to the chair frame. Build up the papier mâché to blend the chair legs and seat together.
5. Paint the chair brown. When dry, use a very thin brush and black paint to create a wood-pattern effect. It is useful to have a piece of wood on hand to look at the lines, knots and patterns that occur in the material.
6. Photograph each child individually in a standing position. A dressing up box with Victorian or ragged clothes for the children to pose in will add to the look of the work if available.
7. Print and enlarge each picture on a photocopier. Add ragged clothing using pieces of felt and lace stuck on to the photocopied figure. Stick to the chair, bending at the knees and waist. Encourage the children to imagine themselves as a Victorian child and to write a speech bubble to attach to their piece.

Resources

- Cardboard 25 x 45cm
- Large paper cups
- PVA glue
- Lolly sticks
- Glue gun
- Tissue paper
- Brown poster or acrylic paint
- Black poster or acrylic paint
- Medium and thin brushes
- Photo of each child
- Felt and lace

Victorian Paper Dolls

Dolls in the Victorian era were created by hand and made of bone china, which meant they were very fragile. They were very expensive to buy and so were usually bought by wealthy parents for their children. The accessible doll made for ordinary children was simple, mass-produced and made of paper. Look at examples of modern 'paper dolls' as a starting point. Also look at images of how children and adults dressed during the Victorian era and discuss the differences in style between now and then. The clothes during the era change a great deal as Queen Victoria reigned for a long period of time.

Resources

- Digital camera
- Stiff cardboard
- Medium-weight card
- Scissors
- Fabric, felt or coloured paper
- Buttons and ribbons
- Paper clips

Approach

1. Make a template for each child by taking a photograph and enlarging each image to A2 size.
2. Cut out the figure, stick it onto a piece of cardboard. Make a standing mechanism by drawing then cutting out a right angle triangle from stiff card and securing to the figure. Cut away the surrounding card leaving the standing figure.
3. Place the figure on the medium-weight card face down and draw around it (excluding the head) to create an outline for the Victorian costume. Draw three flaps on either side of the outline.
4. Draw a Victorian costume over the outline, and cut out taking care not to cut off the flaps.
5. Use the fabric and buttons to decorate the outfit and attach by bending the flaps around the cut-out figure. Support the outfit with paper clips if it is too heavy for the paper flaps.

Victorian House Fronts

Depending on where your school is located, it is useful to start this project with a local history walk where children can see Victorian houses first hand and where they can make observational drawings. If this is not possible in your area, then the children need to complete some research into Victorian architectural features and to develop a sound knowledge of the styles that are used for this period.

Approach

1. Make a sketch of a Victorian house front, incorporating ornamental features of choice.
2. Roll out a smooth ball of clay on the board with a rolling pin to a 'pancake' no thinner than 1cm. Using a ruler, draw and cut out a quadrilateral to the desired dimensions to form the house front. Leave extra space for cutting out a roof and chimney.
3. Using the drawing as a reference, cut the roof, chimney and windows out of the clay rectangle.
4. For the door, carve the shape into the clay and 'draw' on extra features.
5. Add features such as window-ledges, dorma windows and chimneypots by cutting out smaller slabs or cylinders. Stick these on with slip (a mixture of clay and water), taking care to score both the edges that are to be stuck.
6. Plants growing from window boxes can be made by forcing clay through the strainer or garlic press. These need to be stuck on with slip.
7. Carve the brickwork into the clay using a knife. The same approach can be used to make the tiles on the roof. Indenting the tip of a lolly stick into the clay also gives a scalloped tile effect.
8. Once finished, set aside to dry for about four days. The models will then be ready to paint.
9. This is when the houses 'come alive'. It is important to take time painting intricacies such as the variations in the brickwork and subtle colours with fine brushes. Encourage the children to mix their colours first.
10. Once the houses are dry, stick the pre-cut card strip onto the back of each house to form a strut, using PVA glue. Leave these to dry upside down. They will then be ready to display in a row as a Victorian street.

Resources

- Paper and pencils for designs
- Air drying clay
- Clay boards
- Aprons
- Rolling pins
- Range of clay tools, including knives
- Ruler
- Lolly sticks
- Metal strainer or garlic press
- Poster paints in various colours
- Range of brushes (including very fine)
- Palettes
- Water pots
- Rigid card pre-guillotined into short strips
- PVA glue

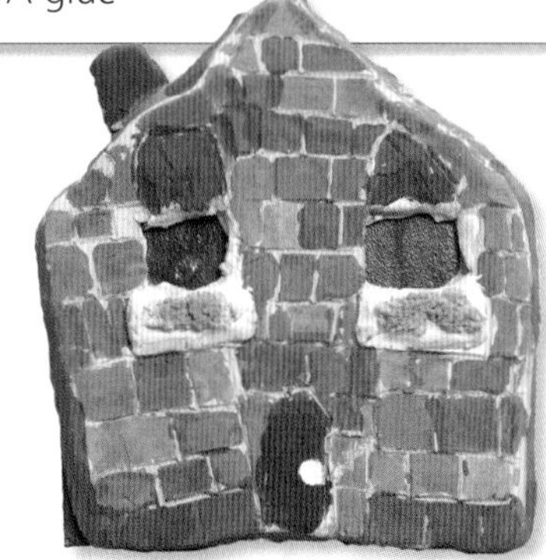

Victorian House Interiors

Generate a discussion around the difference between the houses of the rich and poor Victorians and what features would distinguish the two. Set a challenge for the children to make a Victorian house interior, incorporating features that would be applicable to the type of family living in it. There is not really a step-by-step approach to doing this. When presented with a shoebox and a wealth of materials, the children normally invent their own innovative ways to construct them. Start by asking the children to research the interior features of a Victorian house. Set aside several weeks of classroom activity to create some stunning houses.

Resources

- Shoeboxes
- Card
- Fabric/carpet/wallpaper off cuts
- Paper
- Assorted junk modelling material
- Glue sticks
- PVA
- Spreaders

Approach

1. Divide the shoebox into rooms or floors with card cut to size and stuck with PVA.
2. Decorate the walls with wallpaper off cuts or hand-made wallpaper.
3. Cut out windows if required. Carpet or board the floors with strips of card
4. Furnish the houses in any desired approach, taking care that the furniture is to scale and that the style is appropriate to the class of family living there.

King and Queen Models

Show the children images from the Tudor period including the monarchs painted by Hans Holbein (1497–1543). Photographs of performances of Shakespearean plays are a good source for Elizabethan costume. The Tudor rose emblem together with medieval tapestries show motifs used in textile designs of the period. Linking with life in the Tudor times, discuss the differences in clothing style from what we wear today. Does the type of fabric and level of decoration indicate wealth? Discuss the society of the time and encourage the children to choose a character to dress.

Resources

- Tudor images – people in Holbein's paintings, photographs of Shakespearean plays
- Modelling wire
- Wide dowling or sticks
- Plasticine
- Recycled food containers (e.g. instant noodles)
- Fabric and felt
- Beads, gems, buckles
- PVA glue and glue gun
- Newspaper
- Modroc

Approach

1. To make the figures, place a stick centrally in the plasticine to secure it in a vertical position. Make a hole in the top (adult) of a small container and position the container upside down over the plasticine to act as a base.
2. Use modelling wire to sculpt arms, torso and head (and legs if male).
3. Stuff gaps in the wire with newspaper to bulk out the limbs and body.
4. Use modroc to develop and smooth over the limbs.
5. Once dry, cut fabric and attach by sewing or with PVA (temporarily held with masking tape).
6. Decorate with beads, gems and buckles with glue gun.
7. Optional: it is likely that the children will imagine themselves to be the character they are creating. Add their portrait to the model at the end by photographing each child and attaching each portrait to the face of the model using PVA glue.

Tudor Portraits and Frames

This project is designed to cover a full half term, possibly longer. It can be based upon portraits of children's friends, self-portraits, or paintings of kings and queens. A good starting point is to view Tudor portraits at local galleries or historic houses. Gallery websites also provide excellent examples. Explore how the artists depicted the rich textures of material contrasted with the sombre backgrounds. What is the story behind the face? Do not forget the frames, they are usually just as beautiful!

Resources

- Canvas board or sheet torn out of an A4 acrylic pad
- Acrylic paints (quick drying and easy to use)
- Range of brushes for backgrounds and fine details
- Palettes/water pots
- Light brown coloured pencil
- Aprons (acrylic is hard to wash out)

Approach

Paintings

1. Using a broad brush, lightly paint a wash of burnt umber over the whole canvas.
2. Once the paint is dry, lightly draw the portrait in coloured pencil, taking extra care with the features on the face and the folds and patterns on the clothes.
3. Paint the figure starting with the eyes and working outwards. The idea is to build the painting up in layers. Slowly build up flesh tones and the base colours of the clothes. Indicate dark shadowy areas and highlights. Once the figure is covered, add more detail. If required, deepen and enrich the background, taking care not to encroach on the figure.
4. Add the final touches with a thin brush. At this point, paint in the sparkling highlights in the eyes and on the clothes.

Frames

Resources

- Card
- Ruler
- Pencil
- Gold metallic paint
- String
- Stick-on gems
- PVA
- Scissors

1. Draw and then cut out the frame to the required shape around the outer edge only.
2. Cut the string into pieces, arrange and glue around the frame in a swirling design. Symmetry looks particularly effective.
3. Allow to dry for a few days, and then paint on several layers of gold metallic paint. Make sure each layer is dry before applying a new one.
4. When the frame is dry, diagonally cut the corners of the inner edge and fold the flaps backwards.
5. Arrange and stick on the gems.
6. The frame is now ready to be put on the portrait.

Fabric Dying

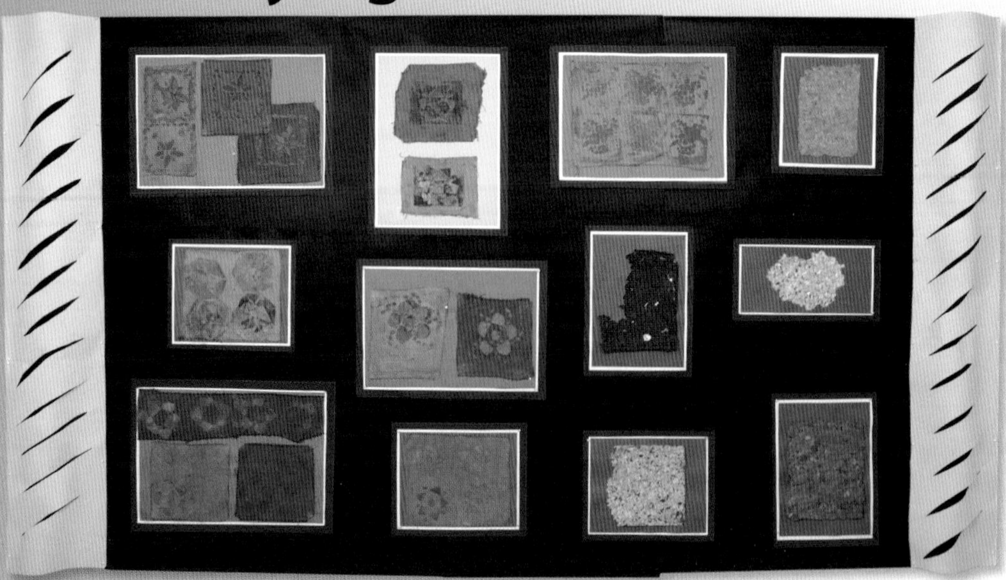

In Tudor times, fabric dyes were made from natural materials such as plants, and even urine and blood! This project replicates the low-tech production of dying fabric in the past, but uses modern dyes. Look at colours worn by Henry VIII and his courtiers, and tapestry designs of the period and select similar colour dyes. Discuss the technology of the period and how materials such as wool, leather, cotton, silk and hessian were utilised by the Tudors.

Approach

1. Follow dye instructions using the warm water and salt.
2. Stir with sticks in the plastic buckets.
3. Squeeze out liquid and flatten to dry.
4. Save for printing activity.

Resources

- White cotton, muslin or hessian in A4-size pieces
- Cold fabric dyes in earthen colours
- 1kg salt
- Plastic buckets
- Warm and cold water

Paper Making

Approach

1. Arrange children to work in pairs to speed up the paper-making process.
2. Tear paper into small pieces. The colours used will determine the colour of the final paper.
3. Fill a bucket with approximately 15cm of water and add a blob of PVA. This will bond the fibres together. Put the pieces in the liquid and stir.
4. Leave the mixture for at least one day and re-tear the pieces to make them into a pulp.
5. In the meantime, prepare the tray by covering with cling wrap.
6. When mixture is pulped, take handfuls and allow the water to drain away. Press out any remaining liquid through the sieve.
7. Carefully spread the pulp onto the covered tray to create a small rectangle of reformed paper.
8. When completely dry, carefully remove from the cling wrap backing and mount paper on a board.

Resources

- Variety of paper in colour and type – crepe, newsprint, sugar, cartridge (the more fibrous the better)
- Plastic buckets
- Water and PVA mix
- Sieve
- Plastic or metal tray
- Cling wrap

Printmaking

Printmaking with poly board is a quick, versatile and accessible way of making pictures. Two sources of visual material are portraits of the Tudors drawn into the poly board and the Tudor Rose emblem. The Rose can be interpreted in very individual ways and become a geometrical project explored by working within a hexagon or octagon design.

Approach

1. For a 'positive' impression, draw separate pieces on the poly block, cut out (adult) and use PVA to place onto another piece of poly block measuring approximately 10cm × 10cm.
2. Once dry and secure, roll on printing ink and press on to paper and/or cold dyed fabric pieces.
3. For a 'negative' impression, draw an image on the poly block surface using a pencil.
4. Roll on printing ink and press on to paper and/or cold dyed fabric pieces.

Resources

- Poly board
- Scissors
- Lead pencil
- Coloured paper or cold-dyed fabric
- Printing ink and rollers
- Surface area – plastic tray, plastic sheet or table surface

Tudor Shoes

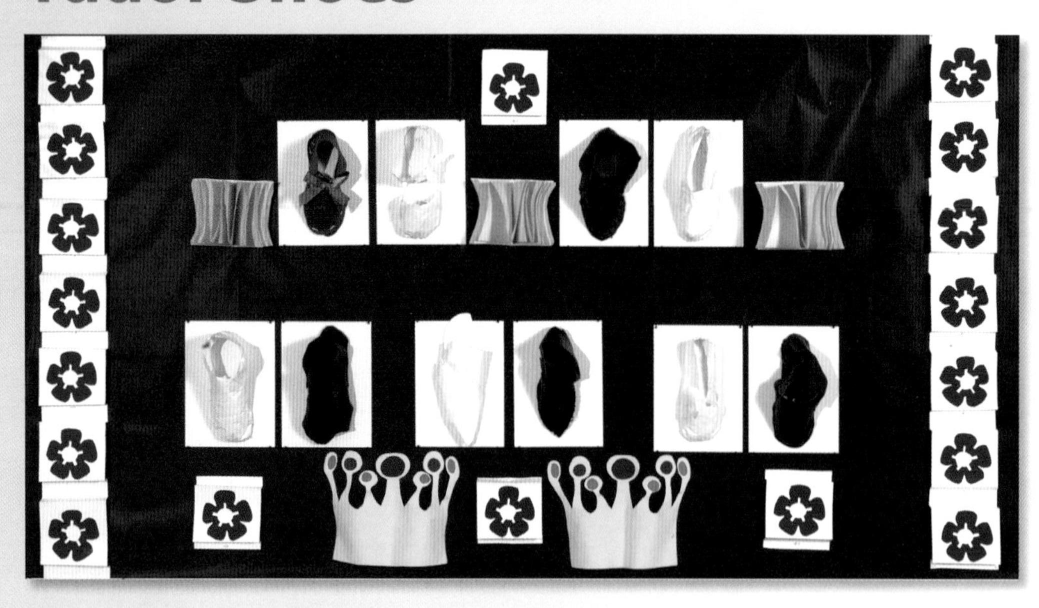

Resources

- Pencil
- White or tracing paper for pattern making
- Leather, plastic imitation, thick fabric, or felt
- Sharp scissors (adult to use if necessary)
- Wire cutters or leather punch
- Ribbon, laces or string

Shoes in Tudor times were very different to those worn today and designing and making your own pair of shoes means reviving a craft of centuries past. Shoes were very simple and this design is made up of a few basic shapes. Select either the two-sided shoe, which is stitched up the front and tied with laces, or the toe-capped shoe, which is more open and tied around the ankle. Please note that these shoes are for display purposes only as they are not strong enough to wear.

Approach

Shoe sole

1. Place one foot flat onto the paper and draw around.Draw another line around the foot outline to give a 1cm gap.
2. Cut along the outer line and this will create the sole.Place the sole on a separate piece of paper, draw around, cut out and turn over. This makes two soles. Mark as right and left.

Two-sided shoe

1. Cut two rectangular pieces of thin white paper slightly bigger than the length and height of one foot.
2. Tape the two pieces together half-way up (like a Cornish pasty). Place over the foot allowing the ankle to come through the untaped part. Attach the two flaps at the back and stick the sides of the shoe to the sole using masking tape to make a paper template of the shoe. Draw on and trim the excess paper to fit the foot. Repeat the process for the other foot.
3. Dismantle the left foot and trim off edges. Lay each piece onto leather or stiff fabric and cut out.
4. Using chalk or a marker pen, mark the perimeter edges with dots 1cm apart for sewing. Make holes through these marks using the wire cutters or leather punch.
5. Sew pieces together starting with the sole and one side, and end with the stitches at the front.
6. Complete by adding laces at the top.

Toe-capped shoe

1. Place one foot on the paper and draw a semi-circle around the toes with 3cm to spare. Cut 1cm darts (v-shaped cuts) from the perimeter, so when semi-circle forms the shoe's cap, the darts will close together.
2. Cut a small rectangle of paper to wrap around and fit the ankle, almost closing at the front though not quite.
3. Cut a thin strip of paper for the tie piece or laces that will join together the ankle wrap piece.
4. To create the right foot, turn over the left foot pieces, draw around and cut out.
5. Continue as per steps 4 to 6 for two-sided shoe.
6. Complete by adding paper tie or a ribbon through the top and front part of ankle section.

Tudor Waistcoats

Resources

- Pencil
- Large sheets of white paper × 2
- A loose sweater or T-shirt to trace around
- Material: leather pieces, man-made substitute, non-fray fabric, felt
- Fabric scissors
- PVA glue
- Large plastic needle
- Wire cutters or leather punch
- Embroidery thread
- Scissors
- Newsprint or thin white paper
- String
- Large needle

Images from the Tudor period including the monarchs painted by Hans Holbein (1497–1543) are a great starting point for looking at Tudor fabric design. Photographs of performances of Shakespearean plays are a good source for Elizabethan costume. This project makes an Elizabethan outfit for any Tudor citizen, with a waistcoat and a fancy ruff to match.

Approach

Waistcoat

1. Lay the T-shirt on the white paper, fold back the sleeves so they are not visible. Draw around the T-shirt using the pencil and cut out the outline.
2. To make duplicate for back of the jacket, place the cut shape onto the second piece of paper, draw around and cut out.
3. Fold the first piece down the middle and cut along the crease to make two front panels.
4. Loosely assemble using masking tape sparingly. Children can then work in pairs to make adjustments to the armholes, collars and the distinct point on the two waistcoat front panels.
5. Separate the pieces again and lay each one onto the chosen material. Draw around with chalk and cut out using fabric scissors.
6. If wished, construct the front using small patchwork pieces of leather or material. These should be directly affixed to the two front panels with PVA and trimmed if overlapping at the edges (it will become a little stiff but compensated by a soft back panel).
7. Make holes 2cm apart in each seam side using scissors, a leather punch, or wire cutters. Sew the seams using embroidery thread and a large needle.
8. Use a strip of leather or fabric as a sash to do up the waistcoat, or brass buttons.

Ruff

1. Take a piece of paper measuring approximately 10cm × 200cm.
2. Fold the strip into pleats a concertina fashion at widths of 5cm.
3. Either pierce a hole through the gathered paper and thread the string through, or use a wide needle to thread the string through.
4. Allow the pleats to open slightly, and wear by hanging around the neck and tying up at the back like a necklace.

Crowns

A visit to see the crown jewels at the Tower of London or a book from the Tower is a good starting point for this project. If such a trip is not possible, look at the monarchs of England through the ages as many crowns were made and passed on through the generations. By creating a tailor-made crown, each child can imagine the life of Queen Elizabeth or Henry VIII or his wives. They can make their own design and even personalise it to include their name.

Resources

- Flexible card strips 2–3cm width/approx 70cm length × 4
- A2 flexible card (in gold or silver or painted)
- Stiff cardboard
- Metallic acrylic paints
- Polystyrene chunks
- Red, blue and green acrylic paint
- Stapler (adult use)
- Pencil
- Scissors
- Glue gun (adult use)

Approach

1. Using one of the strips, cut a headband to size and staple securely. Make the internal structure by crossing further two strips from ear to ear and from front to back. Tape in position and staple to secure. Put to one side.
2. Create the design of the decorative part of the crown in a series of panels. Draw one ornate panel between 15cm and 20cm and cut out. Draw around and repeat several times to fit the circumference of the headband.

3. Cut out and paint all the panels using the metallic paint and put aside to dry.
4. To make the jewels, break up small chunks of polystyrene and paint several in red (rubies), green (emeralds), silver (diamonds) and blue (sapphires). For a little shine, add PVA glue and glitter to the paint and mix in.
5. Once dry, decorate each panel with the jewels, sticking into place with PVA glue. Lay flat to dry.
6. To complete, use the glue gun to securely affix each panel to the headband.

Drake and the *Golden Hind*

Sir Francis Drake 9C1540–C96) and his journey to the new world is tale rich with adventure, danger, exploration and piracy. A hero of the Elizabethan age who brought back treasure, tobacco and spices, he is an exciting character whose adventures on board the *Golden Hind* can be explored through this project.

Resources

- Flexible card or shoebox
- Small containers (boxes or plastic packaging)
- Stiff cardboard
- Gold and silver card
- String, buttons, corks, lolly sticks or balsa wood, wooden clothes pegs, tissue paper, fabric
- Grey or black plasticine or clay
- Powder paint in orange or yellow
- Various colours of poster or acrylic paint
- PVA glue or glue gun (used by an adult for speed)
- Blu-Tack®

Approach

1 To create the hull of the ship, fold a rectangular piece of cardboard in half lengthways without making a crease and sellotape each short opening together. The cardboard will naturally form the shape of a hull. Line the inside of the hull with lolly sticks or strips of wood. Decorate the outside with red, yellow and black as on the original *Golden Hind*. Fill with the objects below.

2. For the deck of the ship, make a removable deck using cardboard cut to the size of the opening of the boat. Build a captain's quarters with flexible card and paint brown.
3. For the cannons, paint several corks in black and glue a black button on one end. Cut three holes in each side of the ship and poke the cannons through securing with glue.
4. For the cannon balls, roll several small balls of plasticine/clay and stack together in a triangle.
5. For the barrels, paint several corks brown and glue on gold or black strips at both ends and in the middle when dry. Glue together in a pile.
6. For the rope, coil string around two fingers, cover with PVA glue and allow to dry.
7. For the treasure chest, paint a small container in brown and sprinkle in coins cut from gold and silver card.
8. For the spices, use PVA glue to stick tissue paper in a small container. Spread PVA glue on top of the tissue and sprinkle with powder paint.
9. For the sailors, dress the wooden pegs with small pieces of fabric and paper. Stand upright using Blu-Tack®.

Journeys to the Unknown

This project sets out to create a map in relief of the 'new world' discovered by the explorers of the 1500s. For a long time people thought the world was flat! But Christopher Columbus changed that idea when he sailed from Spain to unknown worlds and 'discovered' South America in 1492. Many explorers followed in the hope of finding gold and conquering new lands in the name of their king or queen. The two most famous explorers in Britain are Sir Walter Raleigh (c.1552–1618) and Sir Francis Drake (c.1540–c96). As a starting point, look at maps from the 1500s and compare them with a modern map of the Americas, Africa and Europe. Sailors were very superstitious and told many stories of sea monsters that became part of sailor folklore. Fish with wings, whales with two spouts, an octopus with fangs are examples that can bring the map to life.

Approach

1. Draw a map of Britain on the right side of the card, the north coast of Africa to the south and on the left draw an imaginary land (the more inaccurate the better!). In the Atlantic Ocean in between, draw some sea creatures.
2. Tear pieces of newspaper or tissue paper and wet in the PVA mixture. Scrunch up and put where a sculptural form is to build up on each drawing. The sea creatures can be modelled so they appear to leap from the water, and the landmass can include hills, valleys and volcanoes.
3. Once dry, continue to sculpt in more detail using modroc (if available).
4. Paint the sea with a mixture of blues and greens. Acrylic is very quick drying and allows for some interesting surfaces to be created by dappling the paint on or smudging with fingers.
5. Continue to paint the land masses with waterfalls, villages and so on. Paint the sea creatures in bright and fearful colours! For spurts of water, use strips of blue paper.
6. For the compass, cross two lolly sticks and glue onto the plastic circle. Use coloured paper to add N, S, E, W.
7. Make the ships from paper and stick onto the board with PVA glue.

Resources

- Large sheet of stiff card
- Newspaper or tissue paper
- PVA diluted with water in a bowl
- Modroc
- Acrylic paint
- Paper
- Plastic circle (e.g. juice lid)
- Lolly sticks

Shakespeare Story Box

This activity makes an ideal homework or classroom project. It brings together all the information gleaned about William Shakespeare (1564–1616), or any famous Tudor figure, into an exciting visual prop. The brief is to design a story box based on the life and works of the bard. The resources contains a list of suggested items but the children may use any materials they wish so long as these can fit into a shoebox.

Approach

1. The aim is for the children to use their own imaginations to utilise the different resources to fill and decorate the box.
2. Start with some storytelling of perhaps two of Shakespeare's plays using language the children can understand. There are books available to buy. Discuss the characters and the tone of the story (comedy, tragedy). For costume ideas have a look at the Globe Theatre website www.shakespeares-Globe.org.
3. Suggested themes are houses, suitcases or the stage.
4. Relax and give the children a free rein!

Resources

- Shoebox
- Fabrics
- Paper
- Card
- Wire
- PVA
- Various collage media
- Scissors
- Staple gun

Tudor Houses

This is quite a large project that will take several weeks to complete. However, it gives the children a real insight into the skills needed to construct a timber-framed building. If enough time is allocated, the finished result can be amazing.

The children need to have completed research into Tudor buildings and their materials. Explain that they are going to be architects and master builders of their own Tudor village. In groups of four, the children work collaboratively on one Tudor building.

Resources

- Lengths of square dowelling
- Pad saws
- Bench hooks with mitres
- Rulers
- Pencils
- Black ready-mix paint
- Grey/brown coloured card or sugar paper
- Coloured pencils/pens
- PVA or glue gun
- Glue stick
- Scissors
- Split pins

Approach

1. Decide the dimensions of the house in length, breadth and height, and accurately measure four lengths of dowelling that will form the base of the building.
2. Using the mitre on the bench hook, cut the appropriate angles with a pad saw to allow the four lengths to dovetail together. Lay them in the square or rectangle shape and glue together. Using a glue gun is quicker and more efficient than the PVA, but will need adult supervision.
3. Repeat the above process to produce the frame for the ceiling. The children should now have two identical quadrilaterals.
4. Again, using the pad saw and bench hook, cut four equal lengths of dowelling to make the vertical beams. The ends do not need to be mitred. Attach these onto the four corners of the base quadrilateral and then attach the top quadrilateral to the top of the vertical beams. The result should be a cuboid frame.
5. Carefully paint the wooden frame black.
6. Measure four pieces of card to fit on the inside of the timber frame for the walls. The beams look good on the outside.
7. Draw windows and doors on the card and cut out three sides, leaving one uncut. Gently fold back the flap to look like shutters or doors. Colour the doors and window shutters appropriately. Attach a split pin to the door as a door knob.

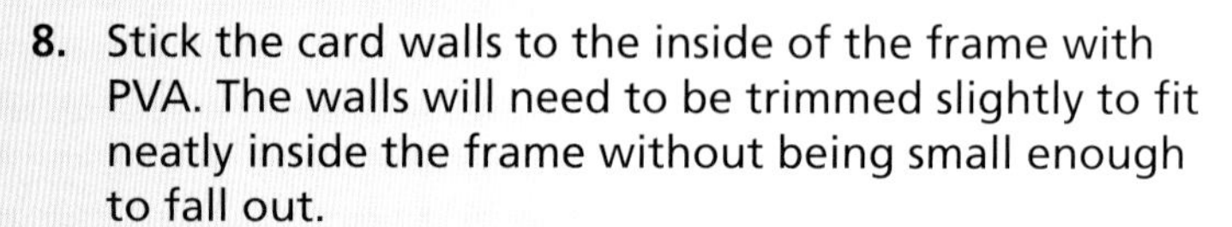

8. Stick the card walls to the inside of the frame with PVA. The walls will need to be trimmed slightly to fit neatly inside the frame without being small enough to fall out.
9. Using the dimensions of the timber frame as a reference, draw a prism net to form an apex roof. This could take a long time as it is quite a tricky task. Set aside a whole session for the understanding and application of making a net.
10. Cut and construct the net and glue into its 3-D shape. Attach the whole roof section to the top of the building using PVA glue.
11. For the roof tiles, cut small squares of grey or brown card and stick onto the roof in overlapping rows, starting from the bottom of the roof and working upwards.
12. Once finished, display the houses as a small village.

Picasso's *Guernica*

Guernica (1957) by Pablo Picasso (1881–1973) is a dynamic and highly expressive mural-sized work that he painted in response to and as a memorial to the bombing of the Basque town of the same name. Basing a piece of work on this famous painting is a good opportunity to look at the work of this famous artist and to demonstrate how other countries, as well as Britain, suffered during the period. The project is made up of several exercises that explore black and white.

Resources

- Charcoal
- Cartridge paper
- Black sugar paper
- Glue stick
- Lead pencil
- Black and white poster paint
- Mixed-sized brushes
- Putty rubber
- Scissors
- Photographs

Approach

1. Begin with a class discussion about the painting, looking at what is going on. There are emotions of anger, fear and despair in the 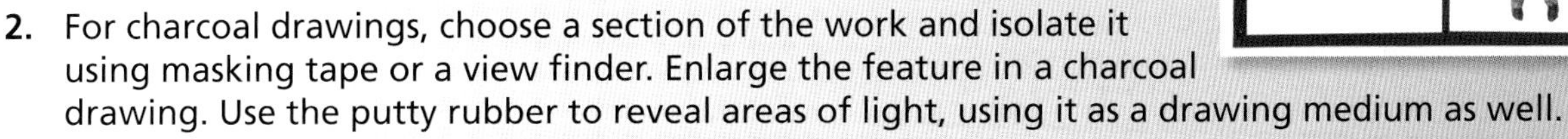 contorted bodies and faces of the people. There are three light sources that may represent hope. The composition of the picture is also key – there is a triangle shape that encloses most of the figures. Diagonals are used by artists to create unease.
2. For charcoal drawings, choose a section of the work and isolate it 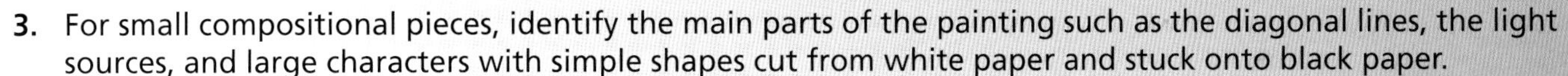 using masking tape or a view finder. Enlarge the feature in a charcoal drawing. Use the putty rubber to reveal areas of light, using it as a drawing medium as well.
3. For small compositional pieces, identify the main parts of the painting such as the diagonal lines, the light sources, and large characters with simple shapes cut from white paper and stuck onto black paper.
4. For black and white tonal mixing, draw several squares on white paper. Leave the first square white and paint the last square black. Using a palette of black and white, mix shades of grey from the lightest to the darkest.
5. For collages, photograph each child standing with arms and legs slightly apart. To create a figure that is experiencing the horror of war, cut each limb at the joint and arrange in a new position.
6. The above exercises come together for the large-scale paintings. Using the collaged figure as reference, draw on a larger scale and paint using black, white and grey.

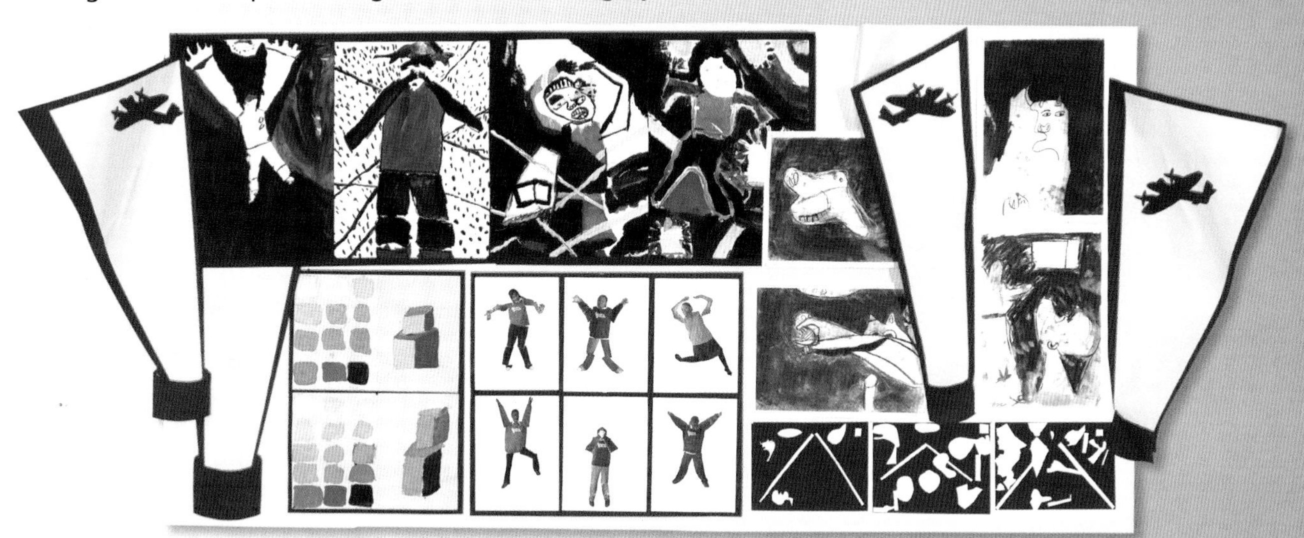

Air Raid Sketches

Resources

- A range of black, beige and ochre sugar paper
- Graphite sticks
- Charcoal
- Brown, white and orange chalk pastels
- CD player, playing wartime music (optional)

Although famous for his sculptures, during World War II, Henry Moore (1898–1986) produced some amazing life drawings of people sheltering in the underground stations from the air raids, such as *Tube Shelter Perspective* (1941). The drawings themselves take on an almost ghostly feel by concentrating on atmosphere rather than fine detail. The faceless figures almost seem to be shrouded like Egyptian mummies. This project is excellent for children to free themselves from the constraints of detail and accuracy by immersing themselves in the whole shapes of the figures they are drawing. With the pressure to 'be right' taken away, the children can enjoy the freedom of making bold, loose lines and atmospheric effects. As a starting point, look at some paintings by Moore and some photographs of air shelters. This project can be used as a one-off stand-alone session.

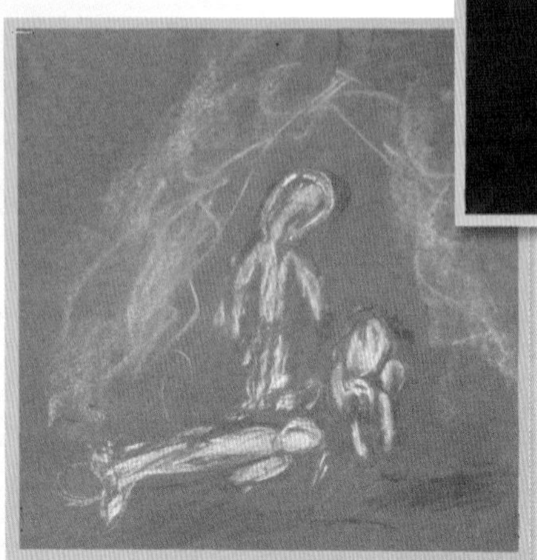

Approach

1. Designate an area to be an underground shelter, have wartime music playing to recreate the feel of the era.
2. Allow volunteers to model, huddling together from the sound of bombs.
3. In short, 20 minute sessions, make quick, loose sketches of the sheltering figures in brown chalk. Concentrate on the whole group, avoiding fine details such as faces. The emphasis is on shape and form.
4. Overlay the figures with orange and black lines, following the contours of the people. This is a good stage to add tones around the figure to suggest a background.
5. Apply white chalk to suggest filtered light highlighting the figures. This seems to make the figures almost spring to life.
6. After 20 minutes stop and choose other models to pose. By the end of the session, the children will be much more fluid and confident in their approach. It is important to keep the drawing sessions short and snappy.

Camouflage Paintings

This is loosely based on World War II as it refers to the camouflage that soldiers would have worn. Of course, in a broader sense, the concept of army camouflage is borrowed from the natural world. This activity can be implemented as an interesting and exciting end to a project of more conventional World War II study.

A good starting point is to view books and images of animals that use camouflage as a natural defence. How effective is the camouflage? How would the children 'hide' themselves in school or in an imaginative world? What would they be hiding from?

As this is a painting exercise that uses small brushes and encourages intricate detail, two sessions need to be put aside to complete the work.

Resources

- Water colour paints
- Good quality watercolour paper cut to A5
- Thin brushes
- Palettes
- Water pots
- Aprons
- Colour images of natural images randomly cut into small rectangles.

Approach

1. Ask the children to choose a colour image. They should try to forget what the picture is of, and instead focus on the colours and shapes that they can see. Ask them to stick the image anywhere on their paper.
2. Using the paints, extend the image outwards, trying to hide the original with clever colour mixing and repetition of the shapes in the original. On no account are the children to paint over the original image (that is cheating). Intricate directional brushstrokes and subtle variations of tone and colour both camouflage and extend the original image.
3. As they work on their painting, the children will begin to paint imaginatively, rather than trying to recreate the image. Echoes of the original colours and shapes will give way to the introduction of new ones. The painting will take on an abstract and surreal feel.
4. At the end of the project, children should view each other's work from a distance and challenge each other to locate the original image in each painting. It never ceases to amaze the children how the painting ends up completely different from what they originally anticipated.

Expressive Clay Heads

During the war people in London took refuge in London underground stations to remain safe during air raids, sleeping in bunk-beds and make-shift hammocks. A starting point for this project is to discuss how children would feel sheltering from the Blitz, being evacuated, hearing bad news from the front or celebrating VE day. This can be extended to imagining scenarios in their own lives that have caused them to feel and express various emotions.

Using mirrors, the children can recall a memory, pull a facial expression linked to the feeling that has been evoked and observe how their features change. They can develop their observations in 3-D by producing a clay head that represents their emotion.

Approach

1. Allocate each child a medium handful of clay. Set a piece aside for use later. To form the head, roll clay into a smooth ball. Use the palm of the hand for a smooth finish and turn the clay as it is being moulded.
2. To create the neck and shoulders, squeeze the lower third of the ball between the thumb and first finger. Mould to produce a neck and shoulders wide enough to support the head. Gently tap the base onto the table and ensure the structure stands without toppling.
3. Shape the head into an oval and smooth out any cracks or bumps.
4. Mix some spare slip (clay and water mix). Demonstrate how ajoined pieces should be scratched or 'scored' and how to apply the slip.
5. To make the eyes, depress two fingers half way down the head to create eye sockets. Roll two pea-sized eyeballs from the spare clay and stick into the sockets using slip. Squeeze the socket around the balls and carve eyelids into the desired expression. Carve or stick on eyebrows and eye pupils using the same method.
6. For the nose, roll a small sausage and place between the eyes, laying it flat to the head. Two small balls flank either side of the sausage's base for the flare of the nostrils. Place another ball between the two nostrils for the nose tip. To shape the nostrils, smooth out all cracks and press a pencil into the two balls.
7. Cut a slit to create a mouth. Make lips by rolling two small sausages and sticking them above and below the slit. Mould into the desired expression.
8. To make the ears, fashion two button-sized discs of clay into kidney shapes and stick to either side of the head. Indent with a pencil.
9. Create hair by scratching or carving into the clay, or sticking on plaits and braids (although sculptures look great bald!).
10. Smooth the skin and mould the mouth, eyes, forehead and cheeks to create subtle facial nuances.
11. To create the underground scene, ask two or three children to lie on a blanket as though asleep and ask the class to make observation drawings. Change children a couple of times to allow everyone to draw.
12. For the body position, choose a sketch and encourage the children to model the clay basing the sculpture on themselves as an underground refugee.
13. Once dry, paint using black, white and grey tones.
14. The sleeping bags can be made of any plain material and sealed at either end with glue or stitching.

Resources

- Air drying clay
- Clay boards
- Range of tools
- Mirrors
- Aprons
- Container of water to make slip
- Black and white poster or acrylic paint
- Diluted PVA glue
- Plain fabric

Artefacts and Matisse-Style Collage

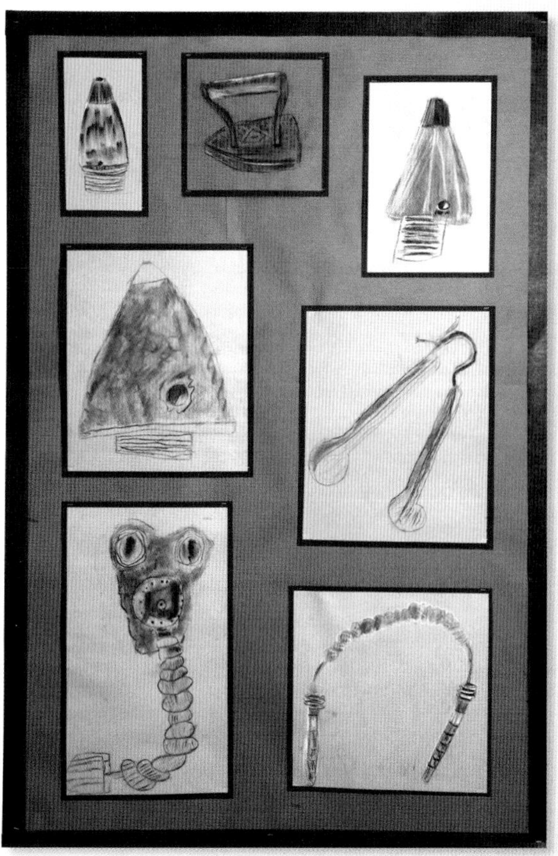

Not every school has access to original World War II artefacts, but some research should amass some interesting 'olden days' artefacts that do not have a military feel. To start this project, it is important for the children to handle and familiarise themselves with the objects before drawing them. Discuss what they think they were used for and how they differ from more modern versions. Discuss the properties of the objects.

Approach

Resources

- Old artefacts
- A3 sugar paper in neutral tones
- Graphite sticks
- Charcoal
- White chalk

1. Loosely and lightly sketch the overall shape of the chosen object, while also applying tone. Tone makes sense of the lines that they are seeing.
2. Gradually build up the drawing by strengthening the lines that the children are pleased with and ignoring any others. Encourage the children to value every line they draw, even those they are not happy with. They are not creating a photo, but an interpretation.
3. As the drawing progresses, select different media to darken the tones. Use white chalk to indicate highlights. It is important to look for shadows cast on the table.
4. Ask the children if they have finished. Knowing when to stop is sometimes hard.
5. Once completed, set up a gallery for other children to come and view.

Paper collage

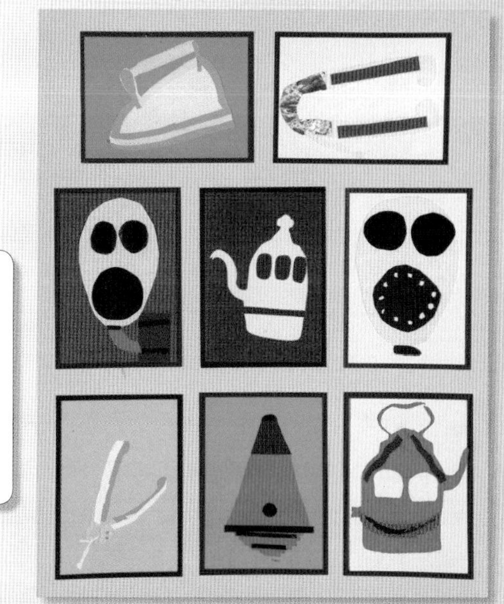

To develop the project, the hildren can use their drawings to create a collage. As a starting point, focus on the paper cut-outs of Henri Matisse (1869–1954). Discuss the use of simplified shapes, the colours that Matisse chose and how a colour is affected when a complementary or clashing colour is placed next to it. Draw attention to the negative space between the shapes and the overall composition of the design.

Approach

Resources

- Range of brightly coloured paper
- Scissors
- Glue sticks

1. Using their drawings as a reference, children select a card in a colour of their choice for the collage background.
2. Cut out elements of the shapes in their drawings onto coloured paper. Encourage children not to use a pencil as the emphasis is not on realism but experimentation.
3. Lay the shapes onto the paper and select colours that either clash or complement. Build the image onto the card and experiment with different colours and placing the various elements of the design.
4. Once satisfied with the image, glue pieces onto the card. Finer details like highlights and shadows may then be applied, but the collages do work well when kept simple.
5. Once completed, mount onto a complementary coloured card and display with the original drawings.

Printed Textiles

Resources

- Pencil
- Poly block and wooden sticks
- Cardboard or small box 15 × 15cm surface
- Scissors
- PVA glue
- Fabric piece approx 70cm × 50cm
- Newsprint paper A1 size
- Printing ink various colours
- Roller and tray
- Card

Benin in West Africa has a strong tradition of textile design.Kente cloths are the traditional textiles woven in Ghana. The togodo/ adanuvo cloths have symbols. Here is a selection with their meanings: bird – merrymaking; butterfly – punctuality; chameleon – patience; comb – grooming and looking good; elephant – kingship; hand – peace; ladder – achieving greater heights; pineapple – friendship; stool – money. This project uses the quick process of printmaking on to fabric, with scope for clothing design.

Approach

1. Cut out and stick a motif to the cardboard square using cut poly block and sticks and a generous amount of PVA glue, allowing at least two hours to dry.
2. While the print block is drying, prepare the mock garment by designing a pattern. Fold the newsprint paper in half length-ways and draw the pattern to be cut.
3. For a V-neck, draw a diagonal line approx 20cm from the central crease upwards to mid-way along the top edge. For a curve neck, follow the same procedure with a curved line.
4. The sleeves require a horizontal line from the outside (open) edge starting approx 20cm down drawn from right to left for 15cm. Continue this line vertically or with a curve to the right. Cut along the drawn lines and open up for a traceable pattern.
5. Lay the fabric on a flat surface. Roll the printing ink onto the block and re-ink for each print to be made.

Weaving

All the clothes we wear are made up of a criss-cross pattern, even if it is really hard to see. Using this principle as a starting point for designing a garment, weaving is an excellent way to both construct the fabric and design a colour scheme at the same time. Printmaking is a further stage in textile design introducing images with symbolic significance.

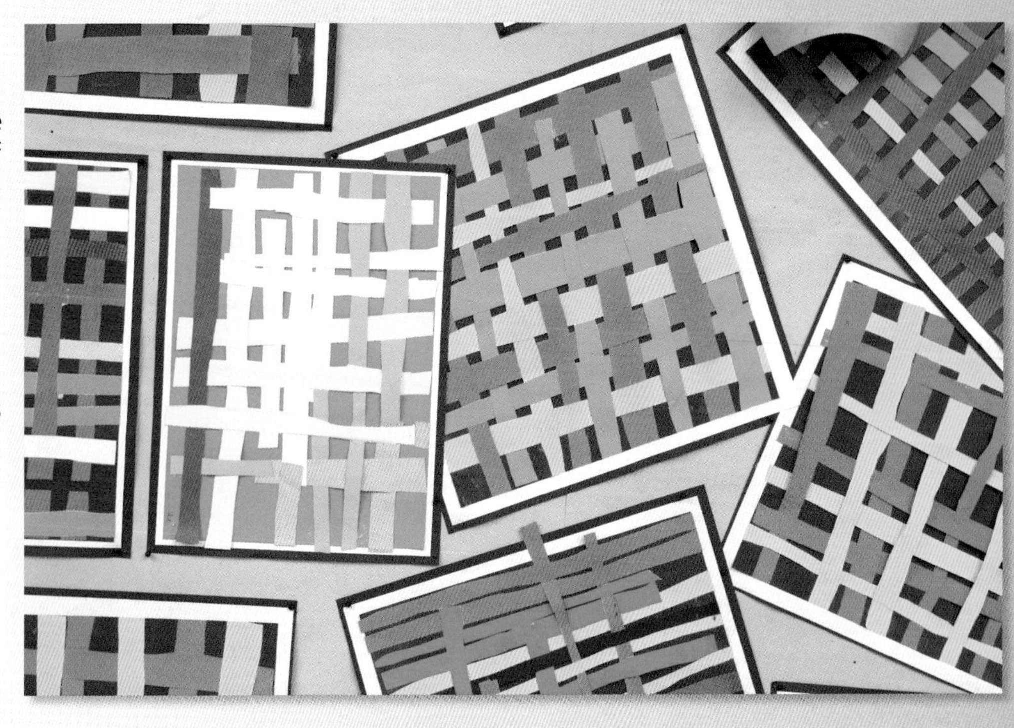

Approach

1. To prepare for the weaving, cut several strips of paper in varying widths (0.5–1.5cm) in 3–5 different colours.
2. Using the glue stick, rub a horizontal line across the top of a black sheet of paper and a vertical line down the left-hand side.
3. Start weaving in the top left-hand corner by placing two strips across one-another. Continue to add one horizontal and one vertical strip, weaving under and over.

Resources

- Black sugar paper 40 × 40cm
- Colour paper A4–A3 size
- Glue stick
- Scissors

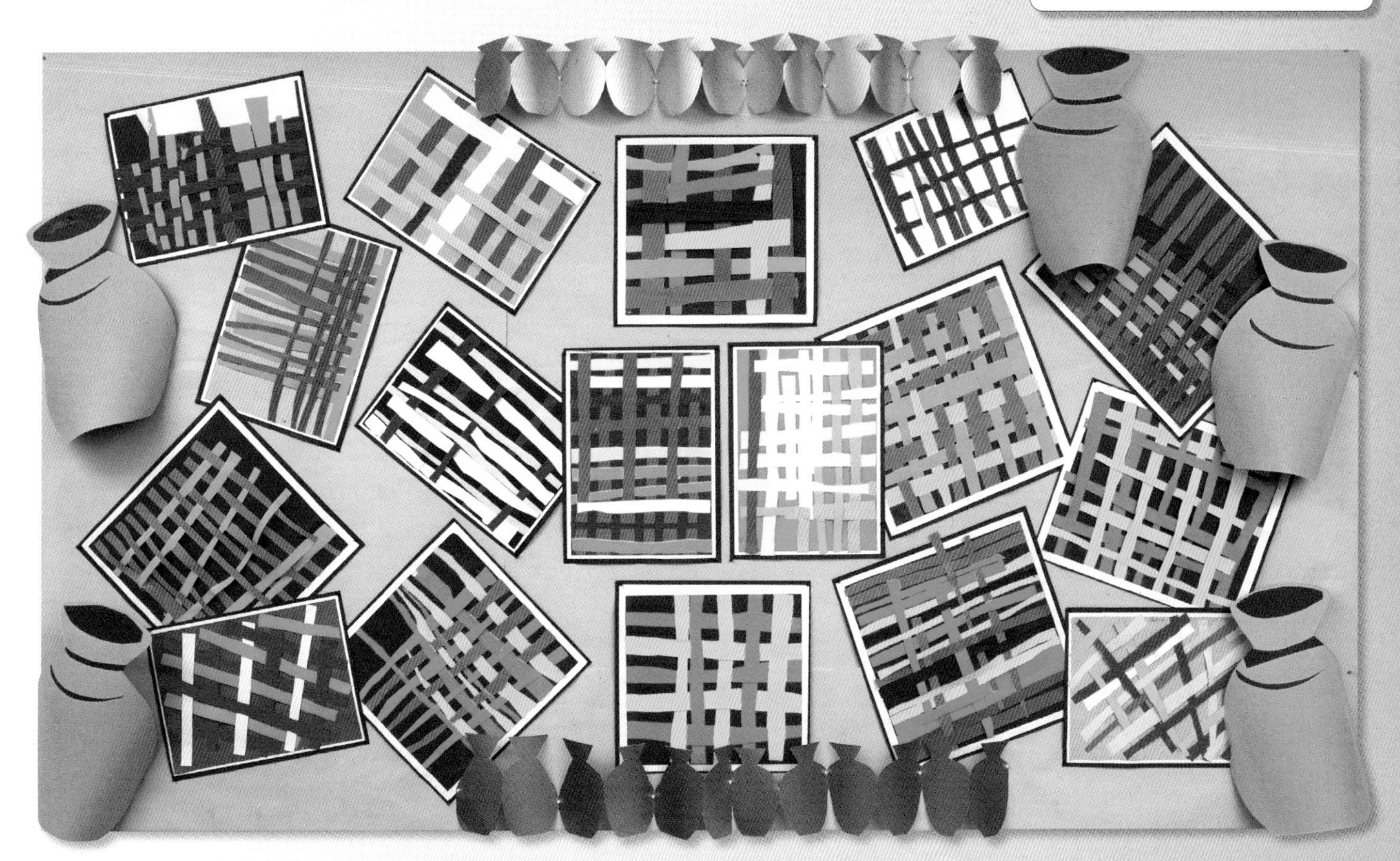

Animal Masks

Mask making has a long tradition all over Africa, the masks in this project are based on animal masks made in West Africa. A good source material for African masks are museums with an ethnographic collection of objects, colour books about African culture, National Geographic magazine and so on. For examples of masks in general, look at the Venetian carnival, even joke shop masks, and discuss their purpose. Disguise, fantasy, hiding, ceremony, ritual are all relevant. The focus of this project is on animal masks. Provide photos of real animals and discuss character traits and the skills each animal could bring to the wearer of the mask.

Approach

Collage

1. Draw a large-scale picture of an animal on the black sugar paper.
2. Focus on the main features of the animal (e.g. shape of features, distinctive markings, colour and texture of fur).
3. Cut, fold or curl paper to build up the face.

Resources

- Black sugar paper A2 size
- Colour paper
- Lead pencil
- Glue stick

Sculpture

Resources

- Thin sculpture wire
- Pliers and wire cutters
- Poly board
- Blu-Tack®
- Modroc
- Container
- Acrylic paint
- PVA glue
- Variety of materials – colour paper, wool, fabric etc.
- Glue gun (adult use)

1. Draw an oval shape on the poly board the size of a face.
2. Cut wire lengths to size and create a criss-cross lattice following the perimeter of the oval drawing. Bend each wire in an arch and attach each end to the drawing perimeter using a lump of Blu-Tack®. Take care not to have big gaps in the wire frame.
3. Cut pieces of dry modroc into palm-size pieces. Wet the modroc and place across the frame building up to at least two layers. Ensure space for the eyes, nose and mouth is left, shaping them and building up the animal features with additional modroc.
4. When the modroc is set, paint a layer of diluted PVA on the mask to create a seal. Use paint to give detail and add material for whiskers, ears and fur etc.
5. To create an African display in the classroom, gather motifs, materials and objects to display with the masks. Batik fabric as worn in West Africa can be found in shops and markets in diverse urban areas. Try your instrument cupboard for drums and shakers. Use books and the internet to source images, and draw and cut out large-scale African objects using card. These will be equally effective.

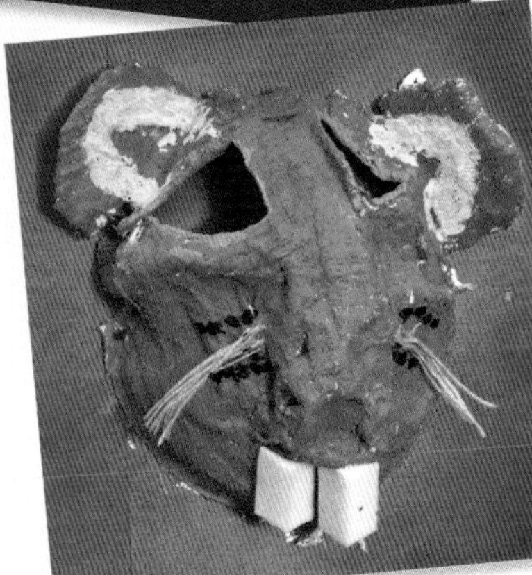

Storytelling Models

This project can illustrate an ancient West African story. The characters shown are from the Nigerian story *How the Crab Lost it's Head* (Kathleen Arnott, *African Myths and Legends*, Oxford University Press, 1990) but any African story involving animals would be suitable. The figures of a crab, two elephants and pond creatures feature in the story. Backdrops can be made using found materials, such as packaging, and decorated by small groups to give the clay figures a context.

Resources

- Clay
- Clay modelling tools
- PVA glue
- Acrylic paint
- Packaging

Approach

1. Read the story and encourage the children to discuss, then research what the setting is like in the story. Many tales involve the land, sea, skies, mountains and villages, and it is a good opportunity for children to learn about a land and climate on the Equator.
2. Create the story backdrop using cardboard and packaging in 3-D. Some characters can become gigantic and it is a stage in the project where children can work in small groups and then assemble pieces once complete.
3. Children can make each character from the story in clay. Once dry, paint with a coat of diluted PVA glue and allow to dry. This creates a varnish and barrier for the paint. Use acrylic paint or poster paint mixed with PVA glue to colour the work. For added protection, add another layer of PVA glue once dry.
4. Arrange the clay figures on the backdrop.

Anansi the Spider

Resources

- Shoebox
- Drawing pencil
- Poster or acrylic paint
- String
- Sellotape
- Tissue or newspaper
- Flexible modelling wire
- Black wool and other colours
- Buttons
- Glue gun
- Small pliers

Choose stories from the past that reflect the location and culture of your school. In this example, the school was based in a multi-cultural area of London and wanted to celebrate culture from Africa and the Caribbean.

Anansi is a vibrant and cunning character who appears in many stories from the Caribbean. Referred to as female or male, this is a clever spider who is often up against oppressive characters or potentially dangerous situations. Anansi's skill lies in an ability to successfully out-manoeuvre opponents and triumph with a sense of quiet justice. This project is suitable for any of the stories you choose.

Approach

1. Paint the interior of the shoebox with the backdrop of the story's setting. It could include other characters, a tropical landscape or the interior of a room.
2. For the legs, use a piece of modelling wire approximately 80cm long, bend it into a row of eight loops with a little to spare. It should look like a series of letter 'm's each approximately 9cm long.
3. This stage will require an adult's help. Use the spare length of wire to weave in and out of the loops, linking them all together, and secure in a knot with the pliers. Bend in the middle to separate, spreading four legs to the left and four legs to the right.
4. Arch the legs to make the structure stand. Put aside to make the body.
5. For Anansi's head and abdomen, screw-up one piece of tissue or newspaper into two adjoining balls. Secure onto the leg frame with wire or string.
6. Add fur to Anansi by wrapping wool around the body section and then each leg in turn. Children may need help tying up the ends upon completion.
7. Create a web for Anansi to hang from by criss-crossing the open side of the shoebox with string and secure with tape. The web does not have a fixed look to it, although point out to the children that spiders work in a spiral, so they could choose to weave.

Grinling Gibbons

Local historical figures are a great starting point for a project that explores the local area. In this example, Grinling Gibbons (1648–1729) was chosen. Gibbons began his career as a woodcarver in Deptford, south-east London, where he made carvings for the ships being built in the docks. St Alfege's church in nearby Greenwich has work by him at the altarpiece, and St Nicolas' church in Deptford has carvings by him. Later he worked for Sir Christopher Wren and his work can be found in St Paul's Cathedral.

He developed a style that was all his own and became famous for carving fruit, leaves, flowers, foliage, fish and birds. These were fixed onto panelling, furniture, walls and even chimneys.

This project was an opportunity for the children to learn about a local historical figure. It began with a visit to a local church where the children made sketches of the carvings they saw. At school, they chose the theme of maritime life (as the school is by the river) and used different materials to work in 3-D.

Dough sculptures

Approach

1. Create a design by drawing separate images on white paper. Cut out, arrange and stick onto black paper.
2. Mix water with the flour to create a springy mixture.
3. Sprinkle a little flour on the table to prevent the mixture from sticking to the surface, and sculpt mixture into desired shape.
4. Bake the sculptures in the oven at 120C or gasmark 1 or 2 until very hard.
5. When cool, paint each sculpture and seal with a layer of PVA glue.

Resources

- Black and white paper
- Pencil
- Scissors
- Plain flour
- Water
- Salt
- Acrylic paint or poster paint mixed with PVA glue

Soap Carving

Approach

1. Create a design by drawing separate images on white paper. Cut out, arrange and stick onto black paper.
2. Soap is a very soft medium to work with and can be carved with plastic modelling tools normally used for clay work.
3. For deep creases, make the groove gradually by working into the area repeatedly. (A deep groove made with force will crumble the soap).

Resources

- Black and white paper
- Pencil
- Scissors
- Bar of soap
- Clay modelling tools

A Temple of Worship

Resources

- Flexible card
- Stiff card (cardboard box)
- Drawing pencil
- Ruler
- Scissors
- Modroc
- Grey/brown poster paint
- Grey/brown paper

The Aztecs lived in what is present-day Mexico, Guatemala, Salvador and Honduras from 1427 to 1521. The Spanish explorer Hernan Cortes arrived in 1519 to a thriving community, but only two years after his arrival the capital was burned to the ground and the empire crumbled because of his greed for gold and power.

Aztec temples were built for worship and based on a triangular design. As a starting point, compare with Egyptian pyramids, drawing particular attention to the staggering of each step with sloping sides. The imposing statue of the temples and their use for ritual and human sacrifice made them an important part of Mayan and Aztec society. This project is best done with groups of four or five.

Approach

1. Ask each group to work as architects and engineers. Their first task is to decide how many layers to have and the measurement of each layer. Steps should be approximately 4cm in height so that each step is staggered, and each layer gets progressively smaller.
2. A step starts like a net for a cube, with a central square and a 4cm flap on each of the four sides. Bend and fold each flap upwards cutting a slight diagonal each corner. When the flaps are joined together they form a trapezium-like shape overall, slanted instead of upright.
3. Cut a piece of card to size to enclose each layer of the temple and seal with masking tape.

4. Using one layer (two maximum) of modroc, cover each step starting with the corners and edges. Add a small room at the pinnacle for the sacrificial hut.
5. Stipple paint with a grey/brown colour that looks like stone and allow to dry.
6. Put together the temple by spreading generous amounts of PVA glue between each layer.
7. For the staircase, cut a width of paper approximately 10cm and fold into pleats in a concertina fashion. Attach to the top and bottom of the staircase.
8. For the final touches, use red paint for the sacrifice and the peak of the temple (optional!).

Cortes and Moctezuma Portraits

The most famous characters from the period of history when the Spanish arrived in South America are the Spanish adventurer Hernan Cortes (1485–1547), and Moctezuma (1466–1520), an Aztec leader. At different stages they were both seen as heroes and took turns at having the upper hand in the battle for Mexico. There are different interpretations of what the men looked like, and it is important to emphasise the artist's role as 'interpreter'. Make a feature of the costume and regalia they both wore as important men.You can find portraits of Moctezuma on the internet, and in children's books on the Aztecs.

Resources

- Pictures of Moctezuma and Cortes
- Poly block
- Scissors
- A4 cardboard
- PVA glue
- A3 cartridge paper
- Coffee granules with cold water and brush
- Drawing pencils
- Black printing ink and rollers
- Colour paper

Approach

1. To create the printing block, draw a picture of the chosen character on the A4 cardboard. Cut the poly board into pieces and glue onto carboard using generous amounts of PVA glue. Put aside to dry.

2. In the meantime, make the antique paper. Tear the edges from the cartridge paper and scrunch the paper into a ball. Unravel taking care not to tear it and flatten onto the table. Brush the cold coffee mixture across the paper turning it a brownish colour like parchment paper.
3. Once the printing block and the paper are dry, set up the black printing ink and rollers. Roll ink on to the printing block, turn over and press onto the paper. (If time allows, practise the printing on some paper before the final print on to the 'antique' paper.)
4. Surround the portrait with gold and silver pieces cut from paper, and add a touch of turquoise mosaic to show the wealth of the Aztecs that was bestowed on Cortes.

El Cortes' Serpent

The Spanish conquistadors arrived in South America in the early 1500s. The most famous was El Cortes (1485–1547), who, on arriving in what is now Mexico in 1519, was thought to be a god by the Aztecs. They presented him with a precious mosaic serpent. This activity transports the maker to the role of Aztec craftsman.

Resources

- Air dry clay
- Modelling tools
- Wooden board
- Rolling pin
- Poster paint mixed with PVA glue or air dry glazes

Approach

1. Remove a small piece of clay from the larger piece for use later.
2. Roll the clay into a long sausage shape the width of a drawing pin approximately 60cm long. Allow the ends of sausage to grow larger as you roll as these will form the serpent's heads.
3. Make a bend in the middle of the sausage pulling the two ends upwards to make a V-shape.

4. Bring the two sides downwards to create an M-shape, pinching a loop to make the first of the five coils of the serpent. Continue bending the roll up and down to make five loops.
5. Use the modelling tools to carve the serpent's two heads, adding fangs and detail.
6. Roll the smaller piece of clay flat using with the rolling pin, and cut out small squares. Place and press the squares on to the sculpture creating the mosaic effect.
7. Use turquoise, black, white and red to paint the serpent. When dry, paint with a layer of watered-down PVA glue to varnish and strengthen.

Feather Headdresses

The feather headdress is a well-recognised form of ceremonial costume for many nations in North and South America. This project is based on the Aztec style and demonstrates the level of attention needed to make a bold piece of costume through the use of style, structure and decoration.

Resources

- Flexible card strips 2–3cm width/approx 70cm length × 4
- A2 flexible card in white or colour
- Sellotape
- Poster paints
- Feathers in variety of colours and sizes
- Stapler (adult use)

Approach

1. Using one of the strips, cut a headband to size and staple securely. Make the internal structure by crossing two additional strips – one from ear to ear, the other from front to back. Tape in position and staple to secure. Put to one side.

2. Take a large feather, brush with paint to cover it completely, place a piece of scrap paper on top and press on to the A2 piece of card. Continue across the paper building up layers of printed feathers, changing the colour if desired. Put to one side to dry flat.
3. Take the last strip and using small feathers in two different colours, glue in a row using PVA. Allow to dry.
4. To assemble the headdress, cut around the feather-printed paper at the top to create a jagged pattern. Position by asking each child to wear their internal structure, and then holding the printed paper across the front of the headband. Carefully remove the structure as one and staple to secure.
5. Place the strip of real feathers along the bottom edge and staple into position.

Eagle Warrior

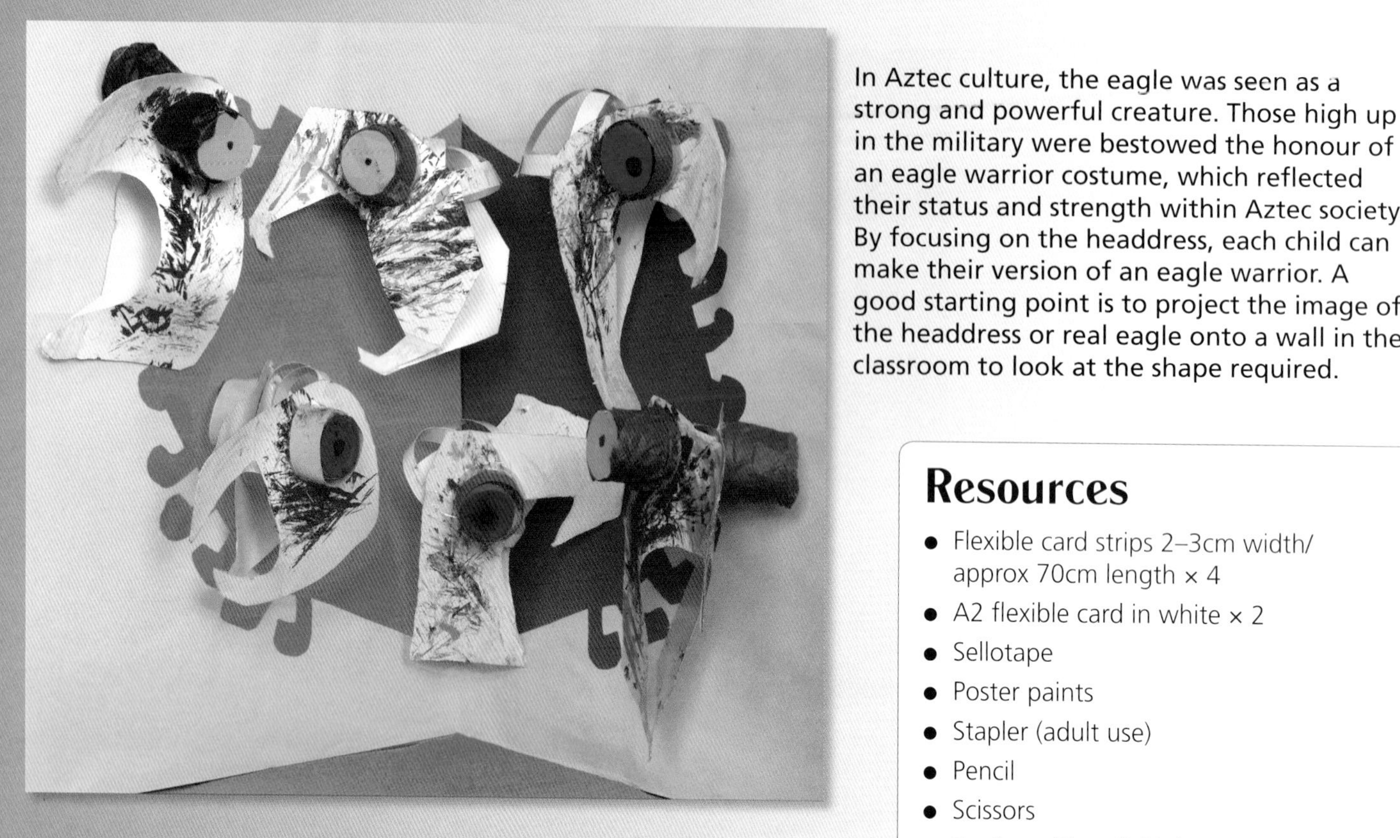

In Aztec culture, the eagle was seen as a strong and powerful creature. Those high up in the military were bestowed the honour of an eagle warrior costume, which reflected their status and strength within Aztec society. By focusing on the headdress, each child can make their version of an eagle warrior. A good starting point is to project the image of the headdress or real eagle onto a wall in the classroom to look at the shape required.

Resources

- Flexible card strips 2–3cm width/ approx 70cm length × 4
- A2 flexible card in white × 2
- Sellotape
- Poster paints
- Stapler (adult use)
- Pencil
- Scissors
- Feathers (if available)
- Poster or acrylic paint in various colours
- Glue gun (adult use)
- Plastic pots × 2

Approach

1. Using one of the strips, cut a headband to size and staple securely. Make the internal structure by crossing two additional strips – one from ear to ear, the other from front to back. Tape in position and staple to secure. Put to one side.

2. Draw the profile of the eagle's head on one piece of the A2 flexible card right up to the edge of the paper. Hold the two pieces together and cut out to produce two equal pieces.
3. Optional: for a feather-effect, take a large feather and brush with paint to cover completely, place a piece of scrap paper on top and press onto the A2 piece of card. Continue across the paper building up layers of printed feathers. Allow to dry.
4. Paint the beak on both pieces of card in yellow.
5. To assemble the warrior headdress, position by asking each child to wear their internal structure, then hold the two sides of paper next to the sides of the headband. Pinch the two sides of the beak together and tape onto the sides using sellotape. Carefully remove the structure as one and staple to secure.

6. For the bulging eyes, paint on or use colour paper on top of the pots (or put paper inside if pots are made of clear plastic). Once dry, use the glue gun (adult use) to secure in position.

Stone Carving

Aztec carvings are usually images that contain a face – either of a god or an animal. For this activity you can suggest to the children the option of carving their own face into the sculpture. It is worth laminating images used for reference to protect them while clay is being used. Before starting, look at the pictures together and discuss the relief sculpture techniques of cutting away clay and building up height for a 3-D effect.

Approach

1. Role the clay flat into a square shape slab approximately W15cm × L15cm × H2cm.
2. Using the modelling tools, draw the outline of the sculpture, then begin to carve away and scoop out low parts of the image.

3. Build up the areas of height using extra clay and model with fingers.
4. Allow to dry and fire in a kiln if using ordinary clay.
5. Use glazes or poster paint mixed with PVA to add colour.

Resources

- Air dry clay
- Modelling tools
- Wooden board
- Clay glazes or poster paint mixed with PVA glue

Cog Montage (Page 39)